C000135615

DARK NLP AND MANIPULATION

Master Your Emotions and Move Freely in the Dark Side of Neuro Linguistic Programming. Protect Yourself from Toxic People and Learn How to Use Mental Control

John Andrew Rough

Table of content

History of Dark Psychology

Dark psychology is the knowledge of a person's state. It includes the psychological nature of people who prey on others with a motive for the crime and deviant behavior, lacking goals and instinctual attraction and social sciences. General assumptions about the theory and all people can harm other people and creatures. Although many people limited or sublimated this trend, some people took measures against these impulses. Dark psychology attempts to understand the system of thoughts, feelings, perceptions and personal processing that lead to predatory behavior contrary to the modern understanding of human behavior. Dark psychology assumes that crime, delinquency and abusive behavior are purposeful and that 99.99% of the time, they have some intellectual, persistent motivation. This is the remaining 0.01% of the dark part of the psychology of Adler's theory and teleology. Dark psychology suggests that there is an area that allows some people to commit violent behavior without purpose in the human mind. This theory is called a dark singularity. Dark psychology believes that humanity has an evil intention to consciously relate to others, from minimal, ambiguous and fleeting thoughts to purely psychopathic deviant behavior, without any coherent rationality. This is called a dark continuum. Dark psychology is called the confounding factor. Softening factor is an accelerator or attractant close to a mysterious singularity. Outrageous human behavior falls on a dark continuum.

A brief introduction to these concepts is as follows. Dark psychology is a concept that has struggled for fifteen years. Only recently, he finally comprehended the philosophy, psychology and determination of the state of man. "Dark psychology is not only the dark side of our moon but also the sum of the dark sides of all satellites." Dark psychology embraces all the people who connect us with the dark side. All cultures, all beliefs, and all people have this well-known cancer. From the moment we are born to die, we all have a hidden side within; some people call it evil, while others are considered a crime, perverted and painful. Dark Psychology introduces a third philosophical concept, arguing that this behavior is different from religious teachings and modern theories of the social sciences. "This is a person who is not interested in his compatriots. The greatest difficulty in their lives is the greatest harm to others. The failure of a person comes from this person." "Dark Psychology" believes that some people will behave the same way, not for the sake of power, money, gender, retaliation or any other known purpose. They committed these terrible acts aimlessly.

Simply put, their end does not justify their means. Some people infringe and hurt others. We all have the potential to harm others without cause, explanation, or purpose in the research field. Dark psychology believes that this dark potential is very complex and even more challenging to determine. Dark psychology suggests that we all have the potential for a predator's behavior and that it can penetrate our thoughts, feelings and perceptions. As you read in this manuscript, we all have this potential, but only a few take actions against them. We all have thoughts and feelings about cruelty. We have dreams of wanting to hurt others cruelly and mercilessly. Although, if you are fair with yourself, you will have to agree with the thoughts and feelings that you thought about committing heinous behavior. Given this fact, we consider ourselves the right kind. I want to believe that we believe that these thoughts and feelings do not exist. Unfortunately, we all have these ideas, and, fortunately, no action was taken against them. Dark psychology consists in the fact that some people have the same thoughts, feelings, and opinions, but manifest their influence intentionally or impulsively.

The apparent difference is that they act on themselves, while others have only short-term thoughts and feelings about it. Dark Psychology believes that the style of this predator is purposeful and has rational, persistent motivation. Religion, philosophy, psychology and other dogmas have made compelling attempts to define dark psychology. Most of the human actions associated with evil acts are truly purposeful, but dark psychology believes that purposeful actions and purposeful motives in the field seem blurred. From thought to pure mental perversion, there is no apparent rationality or purpose, and dark psychology has suffered several injuries. This continuum, the dark continuum, helps to comprehend the philosophy of dark psychology. Dark psychology affects that part of human psychology or the general condition of a person that allows and may even contribute to predatory behavior.

In many cases, some characteristics of this behavioral trend lack obvious rational motivation, versatility and predictability. Dark psychology believes that this general human condition is different or is a continuation of evolution. But let's take a look at some of the basic principles of development. First of all, keep in mind that we evolved from other animals. We are now the model for all animal life. Our frontal lobe makes us a supreme being.

Now, let's assume that the summit's creature does not wholly withdraw us from animal instinct and predatory nature. "The stronger you experience a sense of inferiority, the stronger the desire to win, and the more intense your emotions." Assuming you support evolution, which is true, you think that all behaviors are associated with three basic instincts. Sexuality, aggressiveness, and self-sustaining instincts are the three main motivations for humans. Progression follows the principle of survival of the most adapted and breeding species. We and all other life forms can reproduce and survive. Aggression is to designate our territory, protect our area, and ultimately gain reproductive rights. This sounds reasonable, but in a pure sense, it is no longer part of the human condition. The power of our thoughts and perceptions makes us the culmination of both kinds and cruel practices. And if you've ever seen a nature documentary, you'll surely feel shaken and saddened by an antelope torn apart by the pride of a lion. While cruel and regrettable, the purpose of violence is consistent with the evolutionary model of self-defense. Lions kill the food they need to survive. Male animals sometimes die in battle for territorial ceremonies or the power of the will. All these cruel acts are explained by evolution. "De sees that people always persecute others, but always think that they were persecuted." When animals hunt, they usually hunt down and kill the youngest and weakest women in the group.

Although this reality sounds a little psychotic, the reason for choosing a prey is to reduce the likelihood of injury or death. All animals live to act in this way. All their cruel, violent, and bloody actions are associated with evolution, natural selection, survival and reproductive instincts. You will find out after reading this manuscript, that there is no "dark psychology" application for the rest of the planet. We are people and have what dark psychology is trying to explore. When we study the human condition, it seems that the theories of evolution, natural selection and animal instinct and their theoretical principles disappear. So, we are the only creatures on the planet that hunt each other, and there is no reason for this species to reproduce. Humans are the only creatures that hunt others for inexplicable motives. Dark psychology affects that part of human psychology or the general condition of a person that allows and may even contribute to predatory behavior. Dark psychology believes that there is some inner psychology that influences our actions and is anti-evolutionary. We are the single species that kill each other for reasons other than survival, food, territory or breeding. Philosophers and churchmen have tried for centuries to explain this phenomenon. We'll delve deeper into some of the historical explanations for human malice. Only we humans can have no apparent rational motivation to harm others.

Dark psychology assumes that some are human because we are human, and we promote dark and vicious behavior. As you read, this place or field is common to all of us. Now, before or in the future, no group of people has a dark side. Dark psychology believes that this kind of human condition lacks rationality and logical rationality. And this is part of all of us and has no known explanation. Dark psychology believes that this dark side is also unpredictable. It is unpredictable to know who will act on these dangerous impulses. However, the feeling of kindness towards some people is ultimately denied, and its length will be even more unpredictable. Someone has raped, killed, tortured, and violated for no reason. Dark psychology has demonstrated this behavior. They act as predators in search of human prey without a clearly defined goal. As humans, we are in great danger to ourselves and all other beings. There are many reasons, and dark psychology tries to investigate these risk factors. The more readers can imagine dark psychology, the more prepared they will be, and the less likely they are to fall prey to human predators. And before continuing, it's essential to have at least a minimal understanding of dark psychology. When you finish the future manuscript, this structure will be expanded, and the most important concepts will be presented in detail.

What Is Psychopathy?

The person has a chronic mental disorder with abnormal or violent social behavior. There are several conceptualizations of Psychopathy, including *Cleckleyan Psychopathy* and *criminal Psychopathy* (a meaner, more aggressive, and disinhibited idea entailing persistent and sometimes severe criminal action). The recent conceptualizations are usually used as a modern clinical concept and evaluated using the Psychopathy Checklist. The label "psychopath" can have consequences and stigmatization associated with decisions on penalties for criminal offenses, treatment, civil obligations, etc. Efforts were therefore made to clarify the meaning of the term. The Triarchic model suggests that different concepts of Psychopathy emphasize three observable characteristics to varying degrees. Analisis were made regarding the applicability of measuring instruments such as the Psychopathic Checklist and Psychopathic Personality Inventory to this model.

Courage. Low fear includes stress tolerance, tolerance of ignorance and danger and high self-confidence and social self-confidence. Measures PCL-R is relatively weak, and the main factor is the Facet 1 score. Similar to PPI Fearless dominance. I can correspond to differences in the tonsil and other neurological systems associated with fear.

Disinhibition. Poor impulse control, including planning and foresight, is lacking to influence and invoke authority, demand for immediate gratification, and sparse behavioral constraints. Similar to Factor PCL-R 2 and PPI Pulse antisociality. May correspond to impairments in the frontal lobe of the systems involved in such control.

Meanness. Having no empathy and close affection with other people, contempt for close investments, the use of cruelty to gain empowerment, exploitative tendencies, disobedience of power and destructive excitement seeks. PCL-R is generally related to this, in particular, some elements in factor 1. Similar to PPI, but also includes subscale elements in Impulse antisociality.

Measurement

Early and influential analisis from Harris and colleagues showed that a discrete category, or taxon, may underlie PCL-R Psychopathy, allowing it to be measured and analyzed, and this was just found for the Factor items they identified, the child's behavior problems; adult criminal behavior does not confirm the taxon's existence. Mark, John, and Edens recently conducted a series of statistical analisis on PPI scores. He concluded that Psychopathy might be better positioned as having a "one-dimensional latent structure" like depression. Repeated the study on a more significant sample of prisoners using PCL-R and is looking to exclude other experimental issues that may have previously had different results. They again found that measurement psychopathy does not appear to be a definition of a discrete type (but taxa). They refer that while for legal or other practical purposes an evaluation mark point can be used by arbitrary cut-off, there is no clear scientific evidence of the objective difference point to refer to some people as "psychopaths"; in other words, a "psychopath" can be more accurately described as someone who is "relatively psychopathic." PCL-R was designed for research, not a clinical diagnosis forensic, and even for research purposes to improve understanding of the main issues; it is necessary to study the dimensions of the personality as a whole and not just the constellation of traits.

Personality Sizes

There are different opinions as to what sizes of personality are more important in connection with Psychopathy. Psychopathy has also been associated with high psychoticism, a theorized dimension by referring to violent, aggressive, or hostile tendencies. Aspects related to mental illness include lack of social interaction and responsibility, impulsivity, seeker feeling (in some cases), and aggression. Otto Kernberg, from a particular psychoanalytic point of view, believed psychopathy should be seen as part of the spectrum of pathological narcissism, which ranges from narcissistic personality at the low end, malignant narcissism is in the middle, mental illness is in the high end. However, narcissism is generally considered a possible aspect of psychopathy in the broadest sense. Psychopathy, narcissism, and machiavellianism, the three personality traits collectively referred to as the dark triad, have common characteristics, such as a stale-manipulative interpersonal style. The mysterious notebook refers to these signs with the addition of sadism.

Criticism of Existing Concepts

Modern understanding of psychopathy has been criticized for being underdeveloped, highly subjective, and covering a wide range of underlying disorders. Dorothy One Lewis wrote, "The concept and subsequent reification of the diagnosis "psychopathy" has, to this author's thought, made it challenging to understand crime and violence". According to Hare, in many cases, one does not even need to meet a patient. Just iterate over his entries to determine which items seemed to fit. For this writer of the mind, psychopathy and its synonyms (for example, sociopathy and antisocial personality) are lazy diagnoses. Over the years, the writing team had seen many criminals who, before the authors' assessment, were dismissed as psychopaths. Detailed, psychiatric, neurological, and neuropsychological evaluations have revealed many signs, symptoms, and behaviors that indicate bipolar mood disorder, schizophrenic spectrum disorders. Complex partial seizures, The Half Hare Psychopathy Checklist consists of symptoms of mania, hypomania, and dysfunction of the frontal lobe, often leading to the disorder underlying the dismissal.

The Hare concept of Psychopathy has also been criticized for being a reductionist, dismissive, tautological and ignorant context, as well as the dynamic nature of human behavior. Some call for the abandonment of the concept as a whole due to its vague, subjective, and voluntary life, making it prone to abuse. Psychosis refers to personality traits that have been observed in multiple environments. In moderation, he expresses extensive callous and manipulative self-serving behaviors, oblivious to others, and is often associated with repeated delays, criminality and violence, but can also present himself in other, maybe even successful, social attitudes. Mentally, disturbances in processes related to affect (emotion) and cognition, mainly socially related mental processes, which found in those with the disorder, are indicative of the fact that their destructive social behavior bears from these aberrant mental processes. Developmental, symptoms of psychopathy have been identified in young children with a behavior disorder, and this suggests at least a partial constitutional factor that affects its development.

The Mechanisms Psychopathy

Psychological

Some laboratory studies show a correlation between psychopathy and atypical responses to unpleasant stimuli, including poor conditioning to painful stimuli and sparse learning to avoid reactions that trigger punishment. Hyporesponsiveness of the autonomic nervous system (e.g. skin measurement) conductivity, expecting painful irritant, but not when a stimulus occurs. Although it has been suggested that the reward system is functioning normally, some studies have also shown reduced reactivity to joyful stimuli. According to the response modulation and hypothesis, psychopathic individuals also had difficulty switching with constant action, despite environmental signals signaling the need to do so. This may explain the problem in responding to punishment, although it is unclear if it can explain deficiency conditioning outcomes. There may be methodological questions regarding the research. By setting the average range of idiosyncrasy in linguistic and affective processing under certain conditions, this research program did not confirm the general pathology of Psychopathy.

Neurological

Through the advancement of MRI research, specialists can visualize the specific brain differences and abnormalities in mentally ill patients in controlling emotions and social interactions interaction, ethics, morality, regret, impulsivity and conscience within the brain. Blair, a researcher, the founder of a study on the psychopathic tendencies, stated, "Regarding psychopathy, we have clear indications as to why pathology leads to emotional and behavioral disorders and important ideas in the nervous systems involved in this pathology." Dadds et al. note that, despite the rapidly advancing neurobiology of empathy, little is known about the development of foundations in the psychopathic gap between affective and cognitive empathy. Psychopathy is sometimes associated with brain pathologies in the prefrontal, temporal, limbic regions involved in the emotional and learning processes, among others. Neuroimaging shows structural and functional differences between those who scored high and low on the PCL-R by Skeem et al. that they are "primarily in the tonsils, hippocampus and parahippocampal gyrus, anterior and posterior cingulate gyrus of the cortex brain, striatum, insula and frontal and temporal cortex. " A 2010 meta-analysis showed that antisocial, violent, and psychopathic individuals reduced structural function in the right orbitofrontal cortex, the right front of the cingulate gyrus, and left the dorsolateral prefrontal cortex.

The amygdala and frontal region have been suggested as being of particular importance. People who score 25 or higher in PCL-R, with a corresponding history of aggressive behavior, appear on average to significantly reduce the microstructural integrity between the white matter connecting the amygdala and the orbitofrontal cortex (for example, like a hook beam). The data indicates that the degree of abnormality is primarily related to the degree of psychopathy and may explain the offender's behavior. Also, changes in the amygdala have been associated with "callous-dispassionate" traits in children. The amygdala is also related to positive emotions, where conflicting results in studies in specific areas, may be due to methodological issues. Some of these results are consistent with other studies and theories. For example, in a neuroimaging study, the study of how psychopaths respond to emotional words shows that compared with "normal" volunteers, there is a general difference in the activation patterns of mentally ill criminals in the temporal lobe of the brain, which is different from clinical psychology, the same point of view.

Also, the concept of psychopathy characterized by deep fear is consistent with outcomes of abnormalities in the amygdala, as deficits in aversive conditioning and instrumental learning are thought to be a result of amygdala dysfunction, potentially exacerbated by orbitofrontal cortical dysfunction, although specific causes are unknown. Proponents of the primary and secondary distinction of pychopathy and triarchic models argue that there are neurological differences between these subgroups of psychopathy that support their views. For example, the coefficient of rudeness in the triarchic model is claimed to be associated with decreased activity in the amygdala during scary or aversive stimuli and a decrease in fright reaction. In contrast, the factor disinhibition is argued to be associated with a violation of the frontal tasks of the lobe. There is evidence that insolence and disinhibition are genetically distinguishable.

Biochemical

High testosterone levels combined with low cortisol and serotonin levels were theorized as factors. Testosterone "related to approach-related behaviors, reward sensitivity, reduced fear," and testosterone administration "shifts. The balance of sensitivity from punishment to reward" reduces fear and increases "response to an angry face." High testosterone levels are related to antisocial and aggressive behaviors. Still, other studies show testosterone alone will not cause aggression but will increase the chance of seeking advantage. It is unclear from reviews if psychopathy is correlated with high testosterone levels. Still, several studies have found psychopathy to be associated with low cortisol levels and reactivity. Cortisol increases behavior and reduces sensitivity to punishment and aversion conditions, which is abnormally low in patients with psychosis, and maybe the basis for impaired aversion learning and inhibited expression. Higher testosterone levels and lower serotonin levels can cause "impulsive and highly negative reactions". They can aggravate violent aggression when a person is irritated or depressed. Several animal studies point to a role in serotonergic functioning in impulsive aggression and antisocial behavior.

However, some animal and human studies have shown that the emotional-interpersonal traits and predatory aggression of psychopathy, as opposed to impulsive and reactive aggression, are associated with *increased* serotonergic functioning. A survey by Dolan and Anderson on the relationship between serotonin and psychopathic traits in the personality pattern of disordered criminals found that serotonin functions as a measured prolactin response. In contrast, the inverse relationship between impulse and antisocial traits was positively correlated with arrogant and deceitful characteristics, and, to a lesser extent, a callous and ruthless character. Baris Yildirim theorizes that the 5-HTTLPR, the "long" allele, which is commonly seen as protective against internalizing disorders, can interact with other serotonergic genes to create over-regulation and damping of affective processes, resulting in psychopathy's emotional deterioration. Also, a combination of the 5-HTTLPR long allele and high testosterone levels has been found to lead to a reduced response to threats, as measured by cortisol reactivity. This mirrors the fear deficiency found in those with Psychopathy. Studies have shown other correlations. Psychopathy was associated with an increased ratio of GOK (a dopamine metabolite) to 5-HIAA (a serotonin metabolite).

Studies have shown that people with traits matching the criteria for Psychopathy show a higher dopamine response to potential "rewards," such as money promises or taking drugs like amphetamines. This was theoretically associated with an increase in impulsivity. A great 2D: the 4D ratio of numbers, indicating high prenatal estrogen exposure, there was a "positive correlation of psychopathy in women and a positive correlation of callous influences (psychopathy sub-scale) in men." The results also showed monoamine oxidase A to interfere with the predictive power of PCL-R. Monoamine oxidases (Maos) are enzymes involved in the breakdown of neurotransmitters such as serotonin and dopamine and, therefore, can influence feelings, mood and behavior in humans. The results obtained suggest that further research in this area is necessary.

Common Signs of Psychopathy

Since psychiatric patients are not officially diagnosed, experts refer to the signs described in the ASPD. Masand believes that some of the more common symptoms require attention:

- Irresponsible social behavior.
- Ignore or violate the rights of others.
- Can't distinguish right from wrong.
- Difficulty showing remorse or sympathy.
- The tendency to lie often.
- Manipulate and hurt others.
- Law recurring problems.
- General disregard for safety and stability.

Other behaviors that may be symptoms of ASPD include risk-taking, lure, and deceit that often lie. Masand said that people who exhibit this behavior might also lack deep emotional connections, have superficial charms for them, are very aggressive, and sometimes get angry. People with ASPD don't care whether they hurt others, impulse and abuse, and lack of regret. For ASPD, rudeness does not necessarily mean violence. Masand said that in addition to signs and behavior, ASPD has specific characteristics:

- There are more men than women with this diagnosis.
- Technically, to get an ASPD diagnosis, you must be at least 18 years old. But some people show signs of behavioral disorders as early as 11 years old, which may be an early indicator of ASPD.
- This is a chronic disease that seems to improve with age.
- Due to the behavior of ASPD, its mortality is higher.

Psychopathy Role in Our Society and Culture

There is a limited study of psychopathy in the general work of the population, partly because PCL-R includes antisocial behavior as a significant major (getting PCL-R points above the threshold is unlikely without strong points for the antisocial-lifestyle factor) and does not include positive characteristics of adjustment. Most researchers have studied psychopathy in prison criminals, a relatively accessible population of subjects of study. They may not always have an extensive traditional criminal history or asocial behavior inherent in the conventional concept of psychopathy. Robert Hare argues that the prevalence of psychopathic traits in the business world is higher than among the general population, reporting that while about 1% of the total population meets the clinical criteria for psychopathy, about 3-4% were quoted for senior positions in the business.

Academics on this issue believe that although psychopathy manifests itself only a small percentage of the workplace of staff, it is more common at higher levels of corporate organizations, and its negative consequences (for example, increased hooliganism, conflict, stress, staff turnover, absenteeism, decreased productivity) often causes ripple effects throughout the organization, setting the tone for the entire culture. They can be charming personnel above their level in the workplace hierarchy, helping them rise through the organization, but abusing an employee below their level, and massive can-do damage when they are located in senior management positions. Psychopathy, as measured by PCL-R, is associated with lower performance ratings among corporate professionals

In Fiction

Symbols with psychopathy or sociopathy are some of the most famous characters in film and literature. Still, their characterizations may only vaguely or partially refer to psychopathy, as defined in psychiatry, criminology and research.

The character can be identified as having psychopathies within the artwork, its creators, or the opinions of viewers and critics. It can be based on vague popular stereotypes of psychopathy. Symbols with psychopathic features appeared in Greek and Roman mythology, biblical stories, and some of Shakespeare's works. Such characters are often portrayed exaggeratedly and usually in the role of a villain or antihero, where general characteristics and stereotypes associated with psychopathy are useful in relieving conflict and danger.

As the definitions, criteria, and popular concepts of all of their stories have changed over the years and continue to improve even now. People with mental illness in many famous works at the time of publication can no longer fit the current definition and concept of psychopathy. In both lay and professional accounts, there are several archetypal images of psychopathy that only partially overlap and may include conflicting features: a charming fraudster, a violated serial killer, and a mass killer, with a callous and treacherous businessman, and a chronic low-level offender and juvenile delinquents. The social concept reflects a specific combination of fear of the mythical scarecrow, disgust and intrigue of the surrounding evil, and the passion, and sometimes, perhaps, envy of people who may appear to go through life without investment and unburdened feelings of guilt., melancholy or uncertainty.

What Is Narcissism

Narcissism is the pursuit of vanity or vain worship of idealized self-image and traits, and the word originated from Greek mythology. The fresh narcissus fell in love with his reflection in the pool. Narcissism is a concept in psychoanalysis theory. Since 1968, the American Psychiatric Association has drawn on the old idea of arrogance and listed the classification of narcissistic personality disorders in its "Diagnostic and Statistical Manual of Mental Disorders" (DSM). Narcissism is also considered a social or cultural problem. This is a factor in the trait theory used in various self-report personality scales, such as the Million Clinical Multiaxial Scale. It is one of the three underworld personality characteristics (the others are psychosis and machiavellianism). In addition to the primary narcissism or healthy self-love, narcissism is generally considered to be a problem in the relationship between a person or a group and self and others. Narcissism is different from egoism.

Some Characteristics of Narcissism

- Exaggerated self-importance.
- Lack of empathy, unable to recognize the feelings or needs of others.
- Extreme jealousy and hypersensitivity.
- Focus on a fantasy about beauty, success, strength, and brilliance.

- Arrogant behavior.
- Need constant attention and excessive admiration.
- The tendency to criticize when faced with criticism or lack of attention.

Although narcissistic people cause many problems, they still refuse to change their behavior and attitude. However, narcissists usually attribute these problems to other issues. They even react badly to the slightest criticism or dissent and treat it as a personal criticism. Because of all these negative characteristics, these people find it challenging to maintain healthy relationships with others.

Traits and Signs

Narcissism is four aspects of personality variables: leadership/authority, superiority/arrogance, self-absorption/self-admiration and exploitation/entitlement. Many studies have shown that narcissism has two or more variants, grand narcissism, and vulnerable narcissism. The magnificent variant usually measured by NPI is closely related to the conceptualization of DSM-IV and is a variant related to NPD. NPD is a group B personality disorder that reflects self-importance, entitlement, aggressiveness, and dominance. Status-related characteristics. Fragile narcissism reflects defensive and fragile ambitions, and its function is mainly to cover up feelings of inappropriateness. Fragile narcissism is characterized by allergies, defenses, and withdrawal and is closely related to BPD. BPD is characterized by a fear of abandonment, interpersonal and emotional instability, impulsivity, chronic emptiness, suicidal ideation and self-harm. Pathological narcissism refers to both grandiose narcissism and fragile narcissism, which are related to low self-esteem, lack of empathy, shame, interpersonal troubles, aggressiveness and severe impairment of personality function in clinical and non-clinical samples. Measured according to the "pathological narcissism" list (PNI), pathological narcissism is embedded in personality disorders of border-level organizations, including antisocial, border and narcissistic personality disorders. The PNI scale shows that it is closely related to suicidal behavior, suicide attempts, homicide concepts and the use of psychotherapy.

What Are the Characteristics of Narcissists?

- NPD patients want special treatment.
- They exaggerated their wisdom, success, strength and appearance.
- Lack of empathy allows them to use people without regret.
- Narcissists can be very jealous and very sensitive.

- Since they tend to be thin, they may provoke any criticism or postponement.
- Narcissists may also criticize when they feel that they are not being treated specially.
- Below all these characteristics is a deep sense of insecurity.
- Not surprisingly, when you consider all these characteristics, narcissists may find it very difficult to establish healthy relationships and have a lot of trouble at work or school.

What Causes A Person to Become A Narcissist?

No one knows what causes this disease. It usually begins to appear in adolescents and early adulthood and the factors that cause it are undoubtedly complex. It may be a combination of genetics, neurobiology (that is, how the brain is connected and how it affects behavior and thinking), and the environment (the way people grow).

How Is Narcissism Diagnosed and Treated?

There is no specific test for NPD. The treatment may be painful because narcissists may have difficulty admitting that they have a problem and may view the therapist's usual concession as an attack. However, if they do start psychotherapy and stick to it, this may help bring about a change in attitude and help them understand how their challenging behavior hurts people's lives.

What Is Narcissistic Personality Disorder (NPD)?

The term narcissism has caused a lot of tossing in the culture where we are obsessed with selfies and dominated by celebrities. So, it is often used to describe a person who looks too vain or floods himself. But psychologically speaking, narcissism does not mean self-love, at least not true love. To be precise, people with narcissistic personality disorder (NPD) fall in love with the idealized grand image. The reason why they fall in love with this bluffing self-image is precise that it prevents them from deep insecurity. However, supporting their grand delusions requires a lot of effort, which is where dysfunctional attitudes and behaviors appear. Narcissistic personality disorder involves self-centered patterns, arrogant thinking and behavior, lack of empathy and consideration for others and a great need for admiration. Others often describe people with NPD as arrogant, manipulative, selfish, submissive and demanding. This way of thinking and behavior surfaced in every aspect of the narcissist's life: from work and friendship to family and romantic relationships. People with narcissistic personality disorder try to resist changing their behavior, even if it will cause them trouble. They tend to blame others.

Signs and Symptoms of Narcissistic Personality Disorder

Magnificent Self-Awareness: Magnificence is the defining characteristic of narcissism. Majesty is not only a kind of arrogance or vanity but also a sense of unrealistic superiority. Narcissists think they are unique or "special" and only other extraordinary people can understand them. Moreover, they are too good for any ordinary products. They want to connect with other high-status people, places and things. Narcissists think that they are better than everyone else. They expect recognition, even if they do nothing to gain attention. They often exaggerate or lie about their achievements and talents. When they talk about work or relationships, what you will hear is their contribution, greatness and the luck in people's lives. They are undisputed stars, and everyone else is, at best, a small person.

Live In A Fantasy World And Support Their Grand Fantasy: Since reality does not support their grand views of themselves, narcissists live in a fantasy world supported by distortions, self-deception and magical thinking. They spin the self-glamorizing fantasies of unlimited success, strength, brilliance, attraction and ideal love, making them feel unique and controlled. These fantasies save them from feelings of inner emptiness and shame, so facts and opinions that contradict them are ignored or rationalized. Anything that may break the fantasy bubble will be subjected to extreme defense or even anger, so the people around the narcissist have learned to treat their denial of reality with caution.

Need Constant Praise and Admiration: The superiority of the narcissist is like a balloon, gradually losing air, without continuous applause and recognition to keep it inflated. Occasional praise is not enough. Narcissists need constant food to maintain themselves, so those around them are willing to satisfy their desire for obsessive-compulsive disorder. These relationships are very unilateral, everything an admirer can do for a narcissist and vice-versa. If the admirer's attention and praise have been interrupted or diminished, the narcissist will regard it as a betrayal.

Sense of Right: Because they think they are unique, narcissists expect to be given the treatment they deserve. They sincerely believe that whatever they want, they deserve it. They also hope that those around them will automatically abide by their every wish and whim. That is their only value. If you do not expect and meet all their needs, then you will be useless. If you dare to defy their wishes or "selfishly" ask for rewards, please be prepared for aggression, anger, or indifference.

Use others without guilt: Narcissists have never developed the ability to identify with others' feelings and cannot put themselves in the sight of others. In other words, they lack empathy. In many ways, they view people's lives as objects to meet their needs. Therefore, they will not think twice about using others to achieve their goals. Sometimes this kind of exploitation of interpersonal relationship is malicious, but it is often just forgotten. Narcissists don't even consider how their behavior changes others. So, if you point it out, they still can't get it. The only thing they understand is their own needs.

Often Belittle, Intimidate, Bully, Or Belittle Others: Narcissists feel threatened whenever they encounter someone who seems to lack their things, especially those who are confident and fashionable. They are also threatened by people who do not give in or challenge them in any way. Their defense mechanism is contemptuous. The only way to eliminate threats and support their sagging selves is to suppress these people. They may succumb to prove that the other party does not mean much to them. Otherwise, they may be insulted, bullied, and threatened, forcing the opponent to return to the front and continue to attack.

Don't Be Obsessed with Fantasy

Narcissists Can Be Very Attractive and Charming. They are very good at creating a dreamy, likable self-image that attracts us. We are excited by their apparent self-confidence and lofty dreams, the more unstable our self-esteem, the more attractive the attraction. It is easy to fall into their network, thinking that they will satisfy our desire and make themselves more critical and energetic. But this is just an illusion, and it is costly.

Your Needs Will Not Be Fulfilled (Or Even Recognized). So, it is essential to remember that narcissists are not looking for partners. They are looking for obedient admirers. Your only value is to tell them how great they are to support their insatiable self for narcissists. Your desires and feelings are not necessary.

See How Narcissists Treat Others. If anyone lies, manipulates, hurts, and disrespects others, he will eventually treat you in the same way. Don't be obsessed with your unique fantasy, and they will be spared.

Take Off the Rose-Colored Glasses. Seeing narcissists in your life is crucial to who you are and not who they want to be. Stop making excuses for bad behavior or minimize the harm caused to you. Rejection will not make it disappear. Narcissists are very resistant to change, so the real question you have to ask yourself is whether you can live indefinitely.

Focus on Your Dreams. Don't obsess yourself with the delusions of the narcissist, but focus on what you want. What do you want to change? What fantasy do you need to give up to create a more fulfilling reality?

Set Health Limits

Healthy relations are based on mutual respect and care. But narcissists are not capable of real reciprocity in their relationship. It's not just that they are unwilling; they really can't. They can't see you. They did not receive your message. So, they will not recognize you as someone who exceeds your needs. Therefore, narcissists often violate the boundaries of others.

Moreover, they have an absolute sense of rights in doing so. Narcissists believe that they browse or borrow your property without asking, snoop on your emails and personal letters, eavesdrop on conversations, enter without invitation, steal your ideas and give you unnecessary comments and suggestions without thinking about it. They can even tell you how to think and feel. It is essential to recognize the nature of these violations so that you can establish healthier boundaries based on respect for your needs.

Make A Plan. If you have a model that allows others to violate your boundaries for a long time, it is not easy to take back control. Prepare your success by carefully considering your goals and potential obstacles. What is the most critical change you hope to achieve? Have you tried any methods with narcissists in the past? Not yet? What is the stability of power between you, and how does it affect your plan? How will you enforce the new boundaries? Answering these questions will help you evaluate the options and make a realistic plan.

Consider A Gentle Method. If maintaining a relationship with the narcissist is essential to you, you will have to tread lightly. By pointing out their harmful or dysfunctional behavior, you are destroying their perfect self-image. Try to convey your message calmly, respectfully, and as gently as possible. Focus on how their practice makes you feel, not on their motivations and intentions. If they respond with anger and defensiveness, keep calm. If necessary, please go away and have a conversation later.

Unless You Are Willing to Keep the Border, Please Do Not Set the Edge. You can count on the narcissist to resist new boundaries and test your limits, so be prepared. Follow up any consequences specified. If you step back, it means you don't have to take it seriously.

Prepare for Other Changes in The Relationship. Narcissists feel threatened and frustrated by trying to control their lives. They are used to making decisions. To compensate for this, they may increase demands in other aspects of the relationship, stay away from punishing you, or try to manipulate or attract you to give up new boundaries, this resolutely depends on you.

Don't Do It Yourself

To protect themselves from inferiority and shame, narcissists must always deny their shortcomings, cruelty, and errors. Usually, they do this by projecting their mistakes to others. It is very frustrating to be accused of not being your fault or being blamed for not having negative qualities that you do not possess. However, despite the difficulties, please do not personalize anything to do with you.

Disagree with What the Narcissist Thinks of You. Narcissists do not live in reality, which includes their views of others. Don't let their shame and blame game destroy your self-esteem. Refuse to accept blame, or criticism. This kind of negative emotion is something narcissists must persist on.

Don't Quarrel with Narcissists. When under attack, the instinct is to defend oneself and prove that the narcissist is wrong. Although, no matter how rational you are or how you express your opinions, they are unlikely to hear from you. The point of contention may escalate the situation in a very unpleasant way. Don't waste your breath. Just tell the narcissist that you disagree with their assessment and continue.

You Know Yourself. The best defense against insults and conjectures from narcissists is a strong sense of self. Although you know your strengths and weaknesses, it will be easier to reject an unfair criticism.

Let Go of The Need for Approval. It is essential to be free from the opinions and desires of narcissists to please or comfort them at the expense of oneself. Even if the narcissist has a different view of the situation, you must understand your exact location.

Understand the Look and Feel of a Healthy Relationship. If you come from a narcissistic family, you may not fully understand the healthy supply and demand relationship. Narcissistic dysfunction may make you feel comfortable. Just remind yourself that although it feels familiar, it will also make you feel sad. In a peer-to-peer relationship, you will feel respected, listened to and become yourself freely.

Spend Time with People Who Get Along with You. To maintain perspectives and avoid misunderstandings of narcissist distortions, you must spend time with people who know you and verify your thoughts and feelings.

If Needed, Make New Friendships Outside the Orbit of The Narcissist. Some narcissists isolate people in their lives to control them better. If this is your case, it will take time to rebuild lost friendships or establish new relationships.

Find Meaning and Purpose in Work, Volunteer Service And Hobbies. Don't look for narcissists to make you feel good, but engage in meaningful activities and use your talents and contributions.

How to Leave A Narcissist?

Ending an Abusive Relationship Is Never Easy. Ending a relationship with a narcissist can be particularly tricky. The manipulation of narcissists can easily disorient them, falling into situations where they need to seek their approval, and even feel "surprised" and doubt your judgment. If you are an interdependent person, the desire to be loyal may be more important than maintaining your security and self-awareness. However, it is necessary to remember that in a relationship, no one should be bullied, threatened, or verbally and emotionally abused. So, there are many ways to get rid of the narcissist, internal and self-blame, and start the healing process.

Educate Yourself About Narcissistic Personality Disorder. And the more you know, the more you can recognize the techniques that a narcissist might use to keep you in touch with your partner. When you threaten to leave, the narcissist will usually resurrect the flattery and worship ("love bomb") that made you involved in them in the first place. Otherwise, they will make a bold commitment to change their behavior, and they have no intention of complying.

Write Down the Reason You Left. Knowing why you need to terminate your relationship can prevent you from getting into trouble. Keep the list in a convenient place, such as on the phone, and refer to it when you start to doubt yourself or the narcissist. Could you put it on charm or make weird promises?

Seek Support. During your time together, the narcissist may disrupt your relationship with friends and family or limit your social life. But no matter what situation you encounter, you are not alone. Even if you cannot reach old friends, you can still seek help from support groups or domestic violence hotlines and shelters.

Don't Create Empty Threats. Accepting narcissists will not change; this is a better strategy when you are ready, leave. Warnings or announcements will only warn the narcissist and make it more difficult for you to escape.

Can A Narcissist Fall in Love?

Anyone who loves narcissists will be curious: "Does he love me?" "Does she thank me?" They were torn between love and pain between staying and leaving, but it seemed impossible. Some people swear that they are loved; others believe that this is not the case. It is confusing because sometimes they will meet the caring person they love, and it is a pleasure to be with them. Still, the subsequent behavior makes them feel unimportant or inadequate. And narcissists claim to love their family and partners, but what about them?

How Narcissists Love

Narcissists may show enthusiasm in the early days of dating. However, according to jungian analyst Robert Johnson, this sentiment "always targets our predictions, our expectations, our fantasies... it's not love for another person, it's love for ourselves." This relationship provides positive attention and sexual satisfaction to support the self-esteem of the narcissist. For most narcissists, relationships are transactional. Their goal is to enjoy endless fun. (Campbell et al.) They are playing games and victory is the goal. They are full of energy, full of vitality and have emotional intelligence, which can help them perceive, express, understand and manage emotions. This helps them manipulate people to win admiration. They boast that they are respected, loved and satisfied.

Also, their strong social skills make them make an excellent first impression. So, they can show great interest in romantic prospects and be seduced by promises of generosity, expressions of love, flattery, sex, romance and commitment. Amorous narcissists (Don Juan and Mata Hari types) are skilled and persuasive lovers who may have many conquests but are still single. Some narcissists lie and carry out bomb attacks by overwhelming their prey with words of love, physical and material expressions. Narcissists lose interest when their expectations of intimacy increase or they win a game. Many people have trouble maintaining a relationship for more than six months to several years. They put power in close relationships and prioritize fragility. To maintain control, they avoid maintaining close relationships with others and instead have priority over others. Therefore, playing games has reached a perfect balance, can meet their needs and keep the choice to flirt or date with multiple partners.

A sudden breakup may cause harm to their predecessor, and their forward-looking changes confuse them. The former proposes for one minute and then withdraws for the next minute. They are confused, crushed, abandoned and betrayed. If this relationship continues, eventually, they will see through the seductive face of the narcissist. Some narcissists are pragmatic when dealing with relationships, focusing on their goals. They may also have positive feelings about their partners, but they are more based on friendship and shared interests. If they get married, they will lack the motivation to maintain a romantic facade and take defensive measures to avoid intimacy. They become cold, critical and angry, especially when challenged or unable to extricate themselves. They may meet the needs of their spouses and only need it if it is convenient and self-satisfying. After belittling their partner, they need to find other places to support their high self.

Machiavellianism

It refers to a personality trait, that is, a person is so concerned about their interests that they will manipulate, deceive, and use others to achieve their goals. Machiavellianism is one of the characteristics of the so-called "dark triad. " The other two are narcissism and psychosis. The word itself is derived from a reference to the notorious renaissance diplomat and philosopher Niccolò Machiavelli (Niccolò Machiavelli), his most famous work is "Prince" (Il Principe). This well-known book believed in his view that strong rulers should be harsh on their subjects and enemies. This glory and survival prove that any method is reasonable, even those that are considered immoral and cruel. By the late 16th century, "Machiavellianism" (Machiavellianism) became a buzzword to describe the art of deceptive success. But this is not a psychological term. Until the 1970s, two social psychologists, Richard Christie and Florence L. Geis, developed what they called the "Machiavelli Philosophy Scale." The personality scale is still used as the primary assessment tool of Machiavellianism, and this quantity is known as the "Mach-IV test." Machiavellianism is more prevalent among men than among women. However, it can happen to anyone, even children.

Signs of Machiavellianism

People with characteristics of Machiavellianism tend to have many of the following tendencies:

- Focus only on your ambitions and interests
- Put money and power above relationships
- Charismatic and confident
- Use and manipulate others for success
- Lie and deceive when necessary
- Use flattery often
- Lack of principles and values
- May appear cold or hard to understand
- Good and moral cynicism
- The ability to cause harm to others to achieve its means
- Low compassion
- Often avoid involvement and emotional attachment
- Because of nature, I will be very patient
- Rarely reveal his true intentions
- Prone to sexual intercourse
- Will be good at reading social situations and other
- Lack of enthusiasm in social interaction
- Do not always know the consequences of their actions
- May have difficulty identifying your emotions

Psychological Conditions Related to Machiavellianism

Machiavellianism is considered part of the "dark triad". It is one of the three-character traits, including narcissism and social illness/psychopathy. Each of these characteristics will make someone to try to get along with, so all three aspects that occur in a person may be dangerous to someone's mental health. Although there seems to be an apparent connection between these three "dark triad" traits and the other two unique traits, research is still needed to prove the correlation between the two concretely. The personality disorders that patients may have Machiavellian characteristics include antisocial personality disorder and narcissistic personality disorder. A recent study also found that people with Machiavellian personality have a high prevalence of depression.

How Is Machiavellianism Treated?

The problem with vicious personality traits, as found in the underworld, is that those with such features are less likely to seek treatment or change. They are usually only allowed to participate in therapy if they are encouraged by their family members or if they are told to obey court orders due to crimes. For psychotherapy to be effective, clients need to be honest and allow them to establish a trusting relationship with the therapist. Machiavellianism is the characteristic of a person who is often dishonest and does not trust others. However, as long as you have an experienced psychotherapist, you can make progress. A good psychotherapist with experience of dark triad characteristics will treat each client as an individual and consider its unique history. This will include the conditions they experienced and their unique living conditions. A well-trained therapist can also identify and help treat people with other related problems, such as depression and anxiety. Cognitive-behavioral therapy is a treatment method and is sometimes recommended for people with malignant personality characteristics. It believes that our way of thinking determines our behavior, so by identifying and replacing disordered thoughts and emotions, we can change our behavior.

Features of Machiavellianism

- Focus on their interests and ambitions
- May look charming and confident
- Lack of principles and values
- Avoid emotional attachment
- Put power and money above relationships
- May be patient due to the nature of the calculation

The term "Machiavelli's" is named after the philosopher Niccolò Machiavelli, who believes that the use of immoral behavior to achieve political goals is unacceptable.

The Difference Between Narcissism and Machiavellianism

Narcissism refers to the feeling of being extraordinarily self-centered and self-inflated. At the same time, Machiavellianism refers to the deceptive and manipulative qualities to achieve goals.

Related Qualities: Narcissism is characterized by selfishness, vanity, and lack of compassion, while Machiavellianism is characterized by the exploitation and manipulation of others and lack of morality.

Emotion: The Nazis may quickly anger and criticize, but the Machiavellians may endure because of his computing power.

What Is Machiavellian Behavior?

Machiavellianism is a personality trait that involves manipulative and deceptive, cynical views of human nature, and an indifferent and prudent attitude toward others. Machiavellian describes how individuals adhere to the political philosophy of the Italian writer Niccolò Machiavelli, who advocated concepts involving cunning, deception, and "means to prove purpose." Machiavellianism is one of the three interpersonal personality traits, which together constitute the so-called "dark triad." The other two characteristics are narcissism and psychosis. Compared with Machiavellianism, narcissism involves a grand and exaggerated view of self, superficial charm, and defects in others' thinking.

In contrast, psychosis is a personality trait that requires reluctance, antisocial behavior, lying, cheating, and cruel disregard for others, which may be aggressive and violent. Machiavellianism shares a series of characteristics with narcissism and psychosis called the core of the "dark triad." These characteristics include superficial emotions and wrong emotional attachment to others, self-attention methods for life characteristics, lack of compassion, and low levels of honesty and humility. Machiavellianism itself is a unique feature, and the uniqueness of this feature will be discussed below. The MACH-IV questionnaire usually measures the quality of Machiavellianism.

Indifference to Others, A Caring Point of View

Machiavellians are strategic figures who are willing to lie, and deceive others to achieve their goals. Because of Machiavellian's lack of emotional attachment and shallow emotional experience, little can prevent these people from harming others to achieve their goals. This is one of the causes of why Machiavelli's views and attitudes are so disgusting and problematic. Indeed, similar to psychopaths or narcissists who may hurt others to enjoy their fun, or narcissists who hurt others due to lack of empathy, Machiavellians may manipulate or deceive others into improving themselves, with little consideration for emotional attachment.

Cold Sympathy Vs. Warm Sympathy

There has been a distinction between cognitive and "cold" insights and emotional and "hot" insights. Specifically, indifferent empathy refers to how we think about others, how they behave in specific situations, and our understanding of how particular individuals occur. For example, managers may rely on indifferent empathy to understand the actions that may arise when they provide negative feedback to employees: this may involve defensiveness, disagreement, and ultimately accepting input. The same managers may also recruit enthusiastic empathy and empathize with employees emotionally. For example, "Sarah feels frustrated and embarrassed when I tell her this kind of feedback, so I want to be as close and constructive as possible." In the latter example, the manager's emotional resonance allows her to shape her speech to avoid emotionally hurting employees. A Machiavellian manager may have a solid understanding of employee reactions but fails to empathize with employees emotionally. The result may be that the manager has encountered harsh and unfriendly things and may not realize any emotional harm she may cause.

Evolutionary Benefits

Studies have shown that although some Machiavellianists show insufficient sympathy, others have a good understanding of the emotions and feelings of others, but do not care. Specifically, a subgroup of Machiavellians was found "bypassing empathy." They have a good understanding of the thoughts and feelings that may arise in others due to deception, manipulation, or other ill-treatment, yet fail to curtail their actions in response. This lack of moral conscience in Machiavellians has been seen by evolutionary psychologists as "evolutionarily advantageous" in that they may not be held back by a consideration of others in the pursuit of their goals. However, the question arises regarding how Machiavellians can develop and maintain long-lasting, emotionally satisfying relationships with others if they cannot emotionally resonate or have little concern for others through feelings.

Theory of Mind

The theory of mind introduces the ability to understand and appreciate people's ability to think in unique ways. The method of thinking is different from empathy because it relates more broadly to the goals, desires, and content of a person's thoughts, rather than the instantaneous changes in thoughts and feelings. In theory, Machiavellians must have a reasonably high theory of Mind to understand what drives the behavior of others so that they can manipulate the behavior of others. Research has explained that there is a negative correlation between Machiavellianism, social cooperation skills, and theory of mind, which suggests that these people may not be as successful in understanding and manipulating others as they claim. Therefore, although the characteristics of Machiavellianism may include a series of beliefs and attitudes about managing others, there is no guarantee that such manipulation will succeed.

Behavior Inhibition

According to Gray's theory of enhanced sensitivity, the behavior is driven by two independent nervous systems: the behavioral activate system and the behavioral inhibition system. Behavioral activation systems are associated with "approaching" trends, including extraversion, social behavior, and taking action. In contrast, behavioral inhibition systems are associated with "avoidance" tendencies, such as introversion, withdrawal behavior, and "thinking rather than doing things." Recent evidence suggests that psychosis and narcissism are related to higher levels of activity in the behavioral activation system. In contrast, Machiavellianism is related to more top business in the behavioral inhibition system. Therefore, narcissists and psychopaths are more likely to participate in aggressive behaviors involving behavior and social interaction. At the same time, Machiavellians are more likely to engage in withdrawal behaviors and rely on their thinking and intuition. This is consistent with the cunning tactics of the Machiavellians to manipulate others, rather than aggressively infringing on their rights like the mentally ill.

Alexander

Machiavellianism is related to dyslexia, which describes a defect in naming and understanding one's emotions. Individuals portrayed as being indifferent, isolated from the world, and disconnected from their emotional experiences. The Alexithymia among Machiavellianists may be the product of a reduced understanding of emotions due to a shallow understanding of these emotions or defects in empathy and theory of mind. Regardless of the reason, the evidence shows that Machiavellians are overly aware of others and themselves, and are often out of touch with emotions.

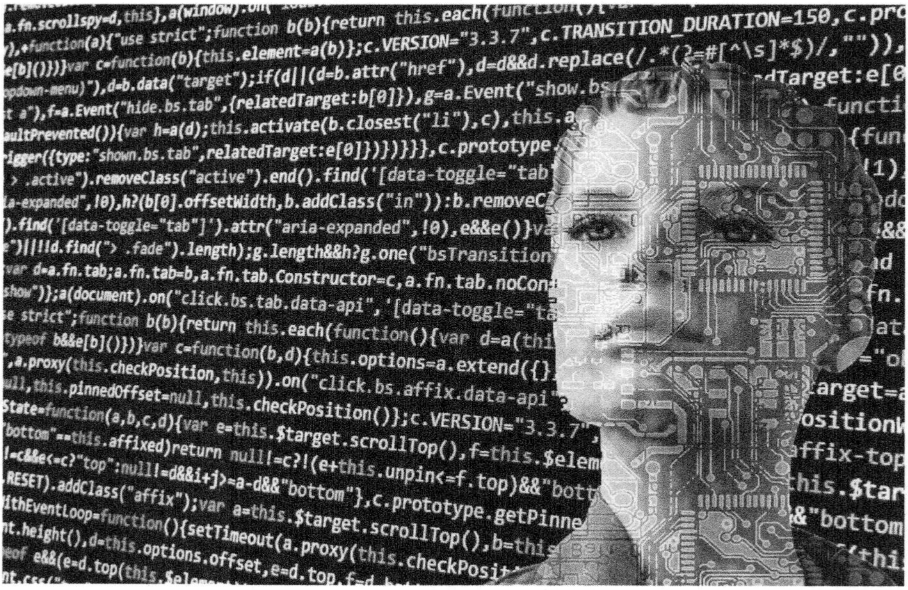

What Is NLP?

Neural Language Programming (NLP) is a pseudo-scientific method for communication and personal development. The creators of NLP claim that there is a connection between neural processes (neurology), language (language), and behavioral patterns learned through experience (programming). They can be modified to achieve specific goals in life. Bandler and Grider also claim that NLP methods can "model" people's extraordinary skills to master these skills. They claim that NLP can usually treat phobias, depression, tic disorders, psychosomatic diseases, myopia, allergies, frequent colds, and learning disabilities in one course. Some hypnotherapists and companies have adopted NLP, and these companies have held seminars as leadership training for companies and government agencies. There is no scientific proof to support the NLP advocates claims, and it has been regarded as pseudoscience. Scientific reviews point out that natural language processing is based on outdated metaphors about how the brain works. This metaphor is inconsistent with current neurological theories and contains many factual errors. The review also found that all supporting research on NLP has major methodological flaws and has failed to reproduce the "extraordinary claims" made by Bandler, Grider, and other NLP practitioners three times the high-quality research.

Use Cases of NLP For Better Understanding of Its Potential

By analyzing large amounts of data to provide better service quality, natural language processing brings exciting opportunities to various industries. This branch of AI is considered to be the key to the ever-increasing amount of data generated by navigating silos. Let us further explore how NLP services can benefit in different areas. The following are some critical use cases of NLP in various industries serving various business purposes.

NLP In Neural Machine Translation: Over the years, neural machine translation has improved the imitation of professional translations. When applied to neural machine translation, natural language processing helps educate neural machine networks. Companies can use it to translate content with less impact, including emails, regulatory texts, etc. Such machine translation tools can speed up communication with partners while enriching other business interactions.

Natural Language Processing in Sentiment Analysis: Sentiment analysis helps to estimate customer feedback on brands and products while adjusting sales and marketing strategies. It is also called opinion mining. Currently, the NLP algorithm can identify emotions of happiness, worry, anger, and sadness. By combining sentiment analysis and natural language processing, marketers will have everything they need to develop feasible strategies and make smart decisions.

NLP Human Resources and Recruitment: Human resource professionals use NLP in human resources to filter out relevant resumes and design job descriptions that prevent prejudice and gender-neutrality, thereby speeding up job seekers' search speed. Also, through semantic analysis, the software can filter a large number of synonyms, so that recruiters can detect candidates who meet job requirements.

Natural Language Processing in Advertising: By analyzing digital footprints in social media, email, search keywords, and browsing behavior, NLP enables advertisers to identify new audiences who may be interested in their products. Even simple keyword matching with regular companies can broaden the scope of advertising channels, thereby helping companies spend their advertising budgets more effectively and use NLP algorithms to target potential customers.

Natural Language Processing in Healthcare: According to Becker, NLP can improve clinical documentation, data mining research, computer-aided coding, and automatic registry reports. In emerging cases, it facilitates clinical trial matching, clinical decision support, risk adjustment and stratified condition classification. For the next generation of progress, NLP supports virtual marking of the environment, calculation of phenotypes, biomarker discovery and population monitoring.

Why Is NLP Difficult?

Just as anyone who has typed the "fun of" I want to talk. When talking with people," natural language processing "still has a way to go, the robot passes the turing test. Although we have made great strides in perceptual computing, language is still one of the obstacles that delicate machines cannot overcome. Recently, Newton hosted a speech in which two NLP leaders from two competing technology giants discussed the latest developments and challenges in applying NLP. The two experts first explained how the machine understands and interprets human language, which constitutes the debate: the first is the transcription device that translates spoken word into verbatim records. The second aspect involves the machine parsing the intent from the complete transcript, mapping the plan to the knowledge graph, and finally using the category identifier to output the response to the user's query. This aspect of NLP enables machines to "understand" human language and respond accordingly. If we already know what to do, why do our phones, Alexa or online chatbots don't know what we're going to tell them?

If It Is A Decision Tree, Please Do Not Call It NLP

Many of the chatbots you interact with today are based on a decision tree structure. You can type keywords or select menu options in the chat, and then follow the path, where each decision prompts the result. One of our experts said: "Most chatbots have limited NLP, I don't call them NLP." Then, he continued to use the Domino's Pizza chatbot to explain. The chatbot can understand a set of predefined keywords suitable for one of its pre-programmed paths, but cannot understand requests made by the Domino customer service team beyond the scope of the predefined methods. For example, if you ask what payment it accepts, it won't understand because it won't process the amount until you enter the location and order request.

Our second expert demonstrated that these "simple" chatbots could generally work in most cases and are usually better than humans in these precise use cases. For example, insurance chatbots are a mobile/tablet friendly format used to essentially select different options-guiding you through the path of solution, choosing one at a time. However, NLP-based overall chatbots are more common. One of our two experts recalled that after the IBM and Microsoft chatbot rogue incidents, developers, and more importantly, their employers funded these expensive programs. They were wary of allowing chatbots never to have parameters and learning through human-computer interaction. Accidents such as Tay's release of racist comments can happen quickly, and their impact on brand equity can be huge. This is why customer-oriented NLP is still very conservative and based mainly on decision trees.

In other words, many enterprise applications today are actively deploying NLP-based robots. Both of our experts reported that today's chatbot with the most interaction was developed by the chinese e-commerce giant Alibaba. In addition to handling customer service, its robot assistant, Alice, can also act as a personal shopper. Alice's function is like a search engine, which can help users find the content they need in a format suitable for mobile devices. She follows two different models upon request. For example, if the user says, "I want to reset the password," the robot follows the knowledge graph or retrieval model (for example, Domino's robot). This applies to all frequently asked questions. However, if the user says words like "I'm looking for chic and slim jeans," Alice uses a combination of knowledge graph and semantic indexing to match the user's intent to a specific product. Due to some ambiguities in natural language processing, this aspect of the robot function is challenging to develop.

Why Is NLP So Difficult?

There are two main reasons why NLP is challenging to implement: humans do not always express their intentions through semantically accurate language, and there are many ambiguities in language. Some examples include:

- Semantics "Gabe invited me to his medical school dance party." What is a "ball" in this case?
- Morphology is a part of a word that can be deconstructed to produce different meanings.
- The intention is vague: "I just came back from New York." What do they want?
- Uncertainty of situation: "Elaina was found at the head of the river." It can be the person in charge of the river (location) or the person in charge of the river.
- Unable to infer the meaning of unknown words from a context like humans.
- Disambiguation-"Jaguar" can refer to cars or animals.

These difficulties will arise even if the machine tries to understand the text that is wholly written and expressed. However, in most cases, the book obtained by the tool is not perfect-full of typos or language or intent. These problems are compounded by speech-in addition to the difficulties mentioned above; the machine must also parse speech, for example, to determine whether someone is saying "I scream" or "ice cream."

No wonder smart speakers still misunderstand or eavesdrop on other conversations as commands.

The Development of NLP Is Imminent

In the past, some years alone, robots have made tremendous improvements in identifying intents, mapping intents to knowledge graphs, and using category recognition to respond. Many robots have also been developed using machine learning through public interaction, including Microsoft's Zo and IBM's Watson. "The key to NLP is data-the more data you collect, the more you can correct algorithm errors and strengthen its correct answers with unlimited data and unlimited calculations; we will have the perfect NLP today." The most critical advancement in NLP is word embedding. Words with similar meanings often appear in similar contexts, allowing machines to learn from large amounts of text on Wikipedia, Twitter, and news sites. This technique can also help machines process unknown words in a way similar to humans-it checks the context of the name and compares that context with other related words to get the meaning.

NLP Techniques That Will Change Your Life

Have you faced any situation that made you feel bad? Maybe you have experienced something that makes you feel frustrated every time. Or, in specific work environments where you must speak publicly, you may feel nervous. You may be shy when you want to contact the "special people" you have been following.

Although these feelings of sadness, tension, or shyness seem automatic or unstoppable, NLP's separation technology can help you immensely.

- Determine the emotion you want to get rid of (for example, fear, anger, discomfort, dislike of a situation).
- Imagine that you can emerge from your body and then look back at yourself and encounter the whole situation from the observer's perspective.
- Note that the feeling has changed dramatically.
- To get an extra boost, imagine that you can float out of your body, look at yourself, and then float out of it again, so you are looking at yourself. This double disintegration should eliminate almost all negative emotions in minor situations.

Reframe the Content

When you feel disadvantaged or helpless, try this technique. The restructuring will accept any negative situation and empower you by turning the meaning of the experience into something positive. For example, suppose your relationship ends. It may not seem very good on the surface, but let's reconstruct it. What are the possible benefits of being single? For example, you are now open to other potential relationships. You are also free to do what you want when you need it. And you have learned valuable lessons from this relationship, which will enable you to have a better relationship in the future. These are all examples of redesign situations. By redefining the meaning of breaking up, you can bring yourself a different experience. In a typical condition, it is natural to panic or focus on fear, but this can cause more problems. On the contrary, diverting your attention, as described above, can help you clear your mind and make responsible and fair decisions.

Anchor Yourself

Anchoring originated from the Russian scientist Ivan Pavlov (Ivan Pavlov), who repeatedly rang the bell while the dog was eating, and experimented with it. After repeated sounds, he found that even if there is no food, he can always ring the bell to salivate the dog. This establishes a neurological connection between the bell shape and the salivation behavior, called a conditioned response. You can use these types of stimuli to respond to "anchor" yourself! Anchoring yourself can help you associate the desired positive emotional response with a specific phrase or feeling. When you choose positive emotions or thoughts and deliberately associate them with simple gestures, you can trigger this anchor when your mood is low. Your senses will change immediately.

1. Determine the feelings you want (such as confidence, happiness, peace, etc.).

2. Determine where you want to fix the anchor on the body, such as pulling the earlobe, touching the knuckles, or squeezing the nails. This physical contact will allow you

to inspire positive feelings at will. It doesn't matter what location you choose, as long as it is the only point of contact, you have no other connection.

3. Think about that time in the past (for example, confidence). Go back to that time mentally, float in your body, see with your own eyes, and restore your memory. Adjust your body language to suit your thinking and state. See what you see, hear what you hear, and feel what you remember. You will begin to feel this state. This is similar to telling a friend an exciting past story. When you "enter" your account, you start to laugh again because you "connected" the story and "relived" it.

4. When you return to the memory, touch/pull/squeeze your selected body area. When you relive your memories, you will feel swelling. When the emotional state reaches its peak and begins to consume, release a little.

5. This creates a neurostimulation response, and whenever you touch, the state will be triggered. To feel this state (for example, confidence), move in the same way back.

6. To make the reaction stronger, consider another memory of your state, then go back and re-experience it through your own eyes and the country in the same place as before. Every time another memory is added, the anchor point becomes stronger and triggers a more positive response.

7. Whenever you need to change your mood, use this technique.

Let Others Like You

This is a straightforward set of NLP techniques, but they can help you get along with almost anyone. There are many ways to build a rapport with others. NLP is one of the fastest and most effective methods. The technique involves subtly mirroring the body language, tone and words of others. People like their person. By cleverly mirroring another person, the brain will emit "mirror neurons," which are pleasure sensors in the brain, to make people like the person who reflects them. The technique is simple: stand or sit on the road where another person is lying. Tilt the head in the same way. Smile when they smile. Reflect their facial expressions. When your legs are crossed, cross your legs. Reflect their voice etc. The key to unconscious rapport is subtlety. If you are too open, the other party may notice consciously, which is likely to destroy the rapport. Therefore, please make your mirror image natural and calm.

Influence and Persuasiveness

Although most of NLP's work is dedicated to helping people eliminate negative emotions, limiting beliefs, bad habits, conflicts, etc., another part of NLP is committed to influencing and ethically persuading others. One of the instructors in this field is a man named Milton H. Erickson. Erickson is a psychiatrist who uses hypnotherapy to study the subconscious (real, scientific stuff, not the silly entertainment hypnosis you see in stage performances). Erickson is very good at hypnosis, so he developed a way to talk to other people's subconscious without anesthesia. He can hypnotize anytime and anywhere in daily conversations. This Eriksson-style hypnosis method is called "conversational hypnosis." This is a valuable tool that can be used not only to influence and persuade others but also to help others overcome fear, limit beliefs, conflicts, etc. unconsciously. This is especially useful when communicating with people who might resist (teens who want to listen or not).

What Is Nonverbal Communication?

The key to success in interpersonal and professional relationships lies in your excellent communication skills. Still, you do not use language but the most nonverbal prompts or "body language." Body language uses physical actions, facial expressions, and manners to communicate nonverbally, usually instinctively rather than consciously. Whether you realize it or not, you will continuously send and receive silent signals when interacting with others. Your nonverbal behavior- the gestures, postures, tone of voice you make, and the number of eye contacts you create will send a safety message. They can reassure people, build trust, attract others to you, or offend, confuse, and disrupt what you are trying to convey. These messages will not stop when you stop talking. Even if you remain silent, you can still communicate through words.

In some cases, what you say and what you communicate through communication body language maybe two different things. When you say one thing, but your body language says something else, for example, if you shake your head in denial, if you say "yes," then the listener may think you are dishonest. When faced with this mixed-signal, the audience must choose whether to trust your verbal or nonverbal information. Since body language is a simple, unconscious language that can convey your true feelings and intentions, they are likely to choose non-verbal information. However, by improving your understanding and the use of nonverbal communication, you can express what you mean and build stronger, more meaningful relationships.

Principles of Nonverbal Communication

Nonverbal communication has a unique history and has an evolutionary function different from verbal communication. For example, nonverbal communication is mainly based on biology, while verbal communication is primarily based on culture. Facts have proved that confident nonverbal communication has the same meaning in different cultures, and no oral communication system has the same universal recognizability. Non-verbal communication develops earlier than verbal communication and has an important survival function in the early stage, helping humans develop language communication later. Although some of our nonverbal communication abilities (such as smell) have lost power with the increase of language ability, other skills (such as paralanguage and mobility) have increased with language complexity. The fact that earlier parts of the brain process nonverbal communication makes it more automatic and involuntary than verbal communication.

Why Is Nonverbal Communication Important?

Your nonverbal communication prompts (that is, the way you listen, look, move, and react) tell you whether the person you are communicating cares about whether you are real and how well you listen. When your nonverbal signals match the words you speak, they increase trust, clarity, and rapport. If they do not, they will develop tension, distrust, and confusion. If you want to be a better communicator, you must become more sensitive to body language and non-verbal cues from others and yourself. Nonverbal communication can play five roles:

Repetition: It repeats and often reinforces the message you have expressed verbally.

Contradiction: It may contradict the message you are trying to convey, thereby showing the audience that you may not be telling the truth.

Substitution: It can replace oral information. For example, your facial expressions usually convey more vivid information than words convey.

Supplement: May add or supplement your verbal information. As a boss, if you tap employees and give praise, you can increase the impact of your data.

Stress: It can emphasize or emphasize speech. For example, a massive hit on the table can highlight the importance of the message.

Types of Nonverbal Communication

The many various types of nonverbal communication or body language include:

Facial Expression. Human faces are incredibly expressive and can convey countless emotions without speaking. Unlike some kinds of nonverbal communication, facial expressions are universal. Facial feelings of happiness, sadness, anger, surprise, fear, and disgust are the same in different cultures.

Body Movement and Posture. Consider how your perception of people is affected by how you sit, walk, stand, or raise your head. The way you move and carry yourself conveys a lot of information to the world. This kind of nonverbal communication includes your posture, position, and subtle movements you make.

Gesture. Gestures are integrated into our daily lives. When conducting animated debates or speaking, you may wave, point, beckon or move your hands, often using gestures to express your thoughts without thinking. However, the meaning of certain gestures can be very different in different cultures. For example, the handwritten OK sign conveys a positive message in English-speaking countries. Still, it is considered offensive in countries like Germany, Russia, and Brazil. Therefore, be sure to use gestures carefully to avoid misunderstandings.

Eye Contact. Since vision is dominant by most people, eye contact is a particularly important type of nonverbal communication. The way you look at others can convey many things, including interest, emotion, hostility or attraction. Maintaining eye contact and maintaining the other's attention, the reaction is essential.

Touch. We communicate a lot through touch. Consider the very different messages of a weak handshake, a warm bear hug, patronage of the head, or the arm's controllable grip.

Space. Have you ever felt uncomfortable during a call because the other person stood too close and invaded your space? Each of us needs physical space, although it varies according to culture, situation, and intimacy. You can use physical space to convey many different nonverbal messages, including privacy and emotion, signals of aggression, or domination.

Voice. It's not just what you are saying. This is how you say. When you speak and listen to you, other people will "read" your voice. Things they need to pay attention to include your timing and rhythm, the size of your voice, tone, and tune, and sounds that convey understanding, such as "ah" and "um." Consider how your tone of voice expresses irony, anger, feelings, or self-confidence.

Can Nonverbal Communication Be Faked?

Many books and websites provide advice on how to use body language to help you. For example, they may tell you how to set up a certain way, sharp fingers, or handshake to show confidence or stay dominant. But the truth is that this technique is unlikely to work. That's because you cannot always control all your thoughts and feelings. Moreover, the more difficult you try, the more likely you are to receive unnatural messages. But this does not determine that you cannot control non-verbal prompts. For example, if you disagree or dislike someone's speech, you can use negative body language to reject that person's message, such as crossing your arms, avoiding eye contact, or slapping your feet. You don't have to agree or even say anything. Nevertheless, to maintain effective communication without putting the other party in a defensive state, you can consciously avoid sending negative signals-keep an open position and try to understand what the other party is saying and why.

How Can Nonverbal Communication Go Wrong?

Your communication through body language and nonverbal signals affects how others perceive you, how they like and respect you, and whether they trust you. Unfortunately, many people send out confusing or negative nonverbal signals without even knowing. When this happens, both the connection and trust of the relationship are broken, as shown in the following example:

Jack: He believes he gets along well with his colleagues at work, but if you ask any of them, they will say that Jack is "dreadful" and "very nervous." It seems that he not only looked at you but also swallowed you with his eyes. If he holds your hand, he will grab it in a hurry, and then squeeze it so hard that it hurts. Jack is a caring person. He secretly hopes that he can have more friends. Still, his nonverbal embarrassment keeps them away from others and limits his ability to improve.

Arlene: She is beautiful and has no problems getting along with qualified men, but it is difficult for her to maintain a relationship for more than a few months. Arlene is funny, but even though she always smiles, she exudes tension. Her shoulders and eyebrows are raised, her voice is harsh, and her body is stiff. Being with Arlene makes many people feel anxious and uncomfortable. Arlene has brought her many benefits, but the discomfort she caused on others has weakened her ability.

Ted: Though he found the most suitable candidate when he met Sharon, Sharon was not sure. Ted looks kind, hardworking, and fluent, but cares more about his thoughts than Sharon. When Sharon had something to say, Ted always prepared wild eyes and rebuttals before finishing his thoughts. This made Sharon feel ignorant, and soon she started dating other men. Ted lost his job for the same reason. He cannot listen to others, which makes him unpopular among many of his most admired people.

These smart, good-minded people work hard to connect with others. Sadly, they are not aware of the nonverbal information they communicate. If you want to teach effectively, avoid misunderstandings, and enjoy an uninterrupted relationship of trust socially and professionally, you must understand how to use and interpret body language and improve your nonverbal communication skills.

How to Improve Nonverbal Communication?

Nonverbal communication is a fast, round-trip process that requires you to concentrate on the instant experience. If you plan to say something next, check your phone or think about other things, you will almost certainly miss the nonverbal prompts. You cannot fully understand the subtleties of what is being conveyed. In addition to presenting yourself fully, you can also improve your oral communication by learning to manage stress and develop emotional awareness.

Learn to Control Stress Now: Stress can affect your communication skills. When you are under pressure, you may misunderstand other people, send confusing or offensive nonverbal signals, and fall into unhealthy knee behavior. Remember: emotions are contagious. If you are unhappy, you may make other people angry and make the situation worse. If you feel stressed, please take some time. Take time to quiet yourself down and then return to the conversation. After you restore your emotional balance, you will be better able to face this situation positively. The fastest and most reliable way to calm yourself down and control stress is to use your senses (whatever you see, hear, smell or touch) or through soothing movements. For example, by viewing photos of children or pets, smelling your favorite scent, listening to specific music, or

DARK NLP AND MANIPULATION

squeezing a pressure ball, you can quickly relax and refocus. Since everyone reacts differently, you may need to experiment to find the most effective sensory experience.

Cultivate Emotional Awareness: To send final nonverbal prompts, you need to understand your emotions and how they affect you. You also need to recognize the feelings of others and the true feelings they imply. This is the source of emotional awareness. Emotional awareness enables you to:

- Read others accurately, including the emotions they feel and the latent words they emit.
- Build trust in relationships by sending nonverbal signals that match your words.
- Respond in a way that shows others that you understand and care.

Many of us lose touch with emotions, especially strong emotions such as anger, sadness, and fear because the church tries to cover up our feelings. However, although you can deny or numb your beliefs, you cannot eliminate them. They still exist and are still affecting your behavior. By enhancing emotional awareness and connecting with unpleasant emotions, you will be able to control your thinking and functioning better.

How to Read Body Language?

Once you have mastered the ability to deal with stress and recognize emotions, you will begin to understand the nonverbal signals sent by others better. The following points are also important:

Pay Attention to Inconsistencies. Nonverbal communication should reinforce what is said. This person is saying one thing, but is their body language conveying another thing? For example, when they shake their heads, they tell you "yes," don't they?

Treat Nonverbal Communication Signals as A Whole. Don't read too many single gestures or nonverbal prompts. Suppose that all the nonverbal signals you are receiving, from eye contact to tone of voice and body language. In short, are their nonverbal cues consistent or inconsistent with their speech?

Trust Your Instincts. Don't ignore your instincts. If you feel that someone is dishonest or has no savings, it may be because the verbal and non-verbal prompts do not match.

Assess Nonverbal Signals

Eye Contact: Is the person making eye contact? If so, is it too tight or, just right?

Facial Expressions: What are their faces showing? Is it expressionless like a mask, or is it emotionally present and full of interest?

Intonation: Is the tone of people's inflection showing warmth, confidence, and interest, or is it tense and blocked?

Postures and Gestures: Is their body relaxed or stiff and unable to move? Their shoulders are tense, raised, or relaxed?

Touch: Is there physical contact? Is it suitable for this situation? Does it make you uncomfortable?

Intensity: Does this person look flat, indifferent, dull, or too high profile?

Time and Place: Is the flow of information flowing? Is the nonverbal response too fast or too slow?

Voice: Do you hear a voice that indicates that the person is interested or concerned?

Use of Nonverbal Communication

There are several different uses of non-verbal communication. Here are some of them:

Modify Voice

Non-verbal communication has an essential influence on the content of the conversation. Modifications include:

- Position of the body relative to other people and things
- Whole-body shape
- Movement of limbs, head, and fingers
- Muscle fretting
- Skin tone and texture
- Pitch
- Phonetic surface
- Speaking speed
- Sweating

- Body odor (e.g., pheromone)

Speech modifiers are especially important when used in conjunction with speech and at critical points in a statement (for example, when forming key points).

Replace Speech

Communication can be completed without speaking:

- Pointing with heels, legs, hands, head or whole body
- Gesturing with fingers, hands, and arms
- Head tilt
- Movement of any combination of 90 facial muscles

The replacement speech can be a direct one-to-one gesture with a clear meaning, or it can be a less conspicuous or conscious action. These signals represent requests, attitudes, and intentions.

Control Dialogue

The conversation is the process of taking turns in the discussion. Non-verbal signals are used extensively in requesting, providing, and managing speakers. This includes:

- Docking to gain control.
- Speak loudly or faster to maintain strength.
- Pause to allow others to join.
- Stop asking others to speak.
- Lean forward and need to speak.
- Look away or move back to indicate that you cannot hear.

Convey Personality and Status

Nonverbal communication extends from physical actions to anything that sends messages. This includes many things about who you are and your suitability for social class; these items include:

- The dress consists of style, neatness, and coordination.
- Personal accessories from jewelry to watches and badges.
- Office and desk space at work, including the size and type of computers and chairs, etc.
- The possessions range from cameras to cars to houses.

Expression of Emotion

Emotions are mainly expressed through nonverbal communication. In this type of communication, voice and body can explain your feelings better than words. If you feel unable to express emotions through words, your language and body language can easily conflict, and the messages sent may be interpreted as stress or deception.

Improve Nonverbal Communication Skills

Strong communication skills can help your personal and professional life. Although oral and written communication skills are crucial, research shows that nonverbal behaviors constitute a large part of our interpersonal communication. The following ways can help you learn to read other people's non-verbal signals and enhance your ability to communicate effectively.

Watch Out for Non-verbal Signals

People can communicate information in many ways, so please pay attention to eye contact, gestures, posture, body movements and intonation. All these signals can convey important information, and this information will not be textualized.

Looking for Inconsistent Behavior

When any person's words do not match their non-verbal behavior, you should pay particular attention. For example, someone may tell you that they are happy when they frown and stare at the ground. Studies have shown that when words cannot match nonverbal signals, people tend to ignore what is said and focus on unexpressed emotions, thoughts, and emotional expressions. When someone says anything, but his or her body language seems to imply something else, it may be useful to pay special attention to those subtle non-verbal cues.

Focus on Tone When Speaking

Your mode of voice can convey a lot of information, from enthusiasm to disinterest to anger. Start to notice how your tone affects how other people respond to you and use your tone to emphasize the ideas you want to convey. For example, if you're going to show a real interest in something, use animated voice intonation to express your enthusiasm. These signals convey how you feel about a subject; they can also help arouse the attention of those who listen to you.

Use Good Eye Contact

Good eye contact is another important non-verbal communication skill. When people cannot see others' eyes, they seem to be evading or trying to hide something. On the other hand, excessive eye contact seems to be confrontational or intimidating. Although eye contact is an essential part of communication, it is necessary to remember; good eye contact does not mean staring into someone's eyes. How do you distinguish correct eye contact? Some communication experts recommend that your eye contact interval lasts four to five seconds. Positive eye contact should be natural and comfortable for you and the person you are talking to.

Ask Questions About Non-verbal Signals

If you are confused by another persons nonverbal signals, don't be afraid to ask questions. It is best to repeat your explanation of what you have said and ask for clarification. An example: "So what you said is..." Sometimes just asking these questions can make the situation more transparent. For example, a person may be sending a specific non-verbal signal because he thinks about other things. By further asking his information and intentions, you may better understand his plans.

Use Signals to Make Communication More Meaningful

Remember, verbal and non-verbal communication will convey information together. You can use body language that reinforces and supports what you are saying to improve oral communication. This is especially useful when giving presentations or talking to a large group of people. For example, if your destiny is to appear confident and prepared during the performance, you will want to focus on sending nonverbal signals to ensure that others see you as confident and competent. Standing steadily with your shoulders back and your feet balanced is an excellent way to posture with confidence.

Look at The Signal as A Whole

Another critical component of excellent non-verbal communication skills involves taking a more comprehensive approach to human communication. A single gesture can represent any number of things or even nothing. The key to an accurate reading of non-verbal behavior is to find signal groups that can enhance the common ground. If you only emphasize one piece of information, you may come to incorrect conclusions about what someone is trying to say.

Consider Context

When communicating with others, always consider the communication situation and environment. In some cases, more formal behavior is required, and the interpretation of these behaviors in any other case may be very different. Consider whether non-verbal behavior is appropriate for the context. If you are trying to improve non-verbal communication, concentrate on matching your signal to the level of formality required by the situation. The body language and non-verbal communication you use at work may be completely different from the signals you send when you go out with friends on Friday. Try to match your non-verbal prompts to the situation to ensure that the message you send is delivered.

Note That the Signal May Be Misinterpreted

Some people believe that a firm handshake indicates a strong personality, while a weak handshake suggests a lack of courage. This example illustrates an essential point about the possibility of misinterpreting non-verbal signals. A weak handshake may ultimately indicate other things, such as arthritis. Always remember to look for behavior groups. A persons overall behavior is far more convincing than looking at a gesture in isolation.

What is Mind Control?

Mind control transfers to a process in which a group or individual "systematically uses unethical manipulation methods to persuade others to obey the manipulator's wishes, which usually harms the man being manipulated." The term has been used in tactical, psychological or other aspect. It can be seen as subverting an individual's sense of control over his thoughts, behaviors, emotions or decisions. Brainwashing and thought control theory was initially intended to explain how totalitarian regimes succeeded in systematically and successfully instilling prisoners of war through propaganda and torture methods. These theories were later expanded and changed by psychologists, including Margaret Singer, to explain broader phenomena, especially the transition to a new religious movement. The third-generation approach put forward by Ben Zablocki, focuses on the use of psychological control to retain NRM and cult members. The suggestion that NRM uses mental control technology has caused scientific and legal controversy.

Some Mental Control Techniques

These thought control techniques are subtle and slow. In other words, they will not take effect immediately. Mind control is a long process that will gradually change the victims mind. It depends on the technology used, the duration of the application, and the personal and social factors involved in the manipulation. Also, the application of mind control technology does not require physical force. However, the victims are under considerable psychological and social pressure. Anyone is susceptible to mind control. That is the danger of misuse of manipulation technology. Some of the most popular and effective forms of manipulation are:

- Complete or partial isolation from the family or social core. Due to the full or partial reliance on the manipulator, cutting off the emotional bonds of possible victims helps to control the mind.

- Moderate physical exertion. Some activities are used to weaken the physical and cognitive abilities of the victims, such as forced labor or exercise for too long.

- Change your diet. Sudden changes in diet, especially the reduction of protein, also weaken the body and mind of possible victims.

- Keep reminding you of simple or complex ideas. This is one of the essential techniques because mind control can only work if the plans that are to be inserted into the victim's mind are put into practice. It may be verbal, using songs, spells, or words, with symbols and must-read content.

- Excessive expression of emotion and reward and the robot has paid a lot of attention and rewarded the victims as long as they do something that helps brainwash. All this creates a dependence between the victim and the manipulator.

- Subtle or direct use of drugs and the use of anesthetics is not always present, but it can promote mind control.
- Hypnosis. Make the victim's mind fragile and promote the manipulation process itself.

What Is NLP Mind Control?

Neural Language Programming provides some practical ways to change the way you think, view past events, and process your life. Neural language programming shows you how to control your thoughts and, thus, your life. Unlike psychological analysis that focuses on "why," natural language processing is practical and focuses on "methods."

The development process of NLP: NLP was co-founded by Richard Bandler. He noticed that traditional psychotherapy techniques were not always effective and were interested in trying different ways. He worked closely with Virginia Satir, a very successful therapist, and NLP was born from the technology of working with patients and others.

Control Your Mind: The Principle Behind NLP

NLP has played a role from the beginning, you may not be able to control too much in your life, but you can always control everything that happens in your mind. Your thoughts, feelings, and emotions are not what you already have, but what you want to do. Their reasons are usually involved, such as involving comments or beliefs of your parents, teachers or incidents you have encountered. NLP shows you how to control these beliefs and influences. Using thinking techniques like visualization, you can change your perceptions and feelings about past events, fears, and even phobias.

The Power of Faith

What you believe in can be very powerful. If you think you are sick and dying, then you might be: Doctor Witch has used this technique for hundreds of years. Likewise, if you feel you have something that can make you better, you will usually become better. This "placebo effect" has been thoroughly proven in clinical trials. It boils down to, if you believe you can do something, then maybe you can. But you can also challenge limiting beliefs and change whether you think you can do something by asking yourself the following questions:

- How do I know I can't do it?
- Who told me they might be wrong?

Target Setting

We are all familiar with goal setting principles. Still, NLP has put forward some interesting new insights, focusing on satisfaction rather than dissatisfaction. For example, it helps you achieve positive goals; focus on what you want to have, not what you want to lose. If you still want to know what you want, this will help. For example, instead of buying the house of your dreams, you want to live in it. It's much easier to motivate your satisfying goals.

Mind Control Technology for A Better Life

Our mind is powerful, but we can use mind control technology to control it. We can plant specific thoughts in our minds, and feel the emotions associated with that thought, and train your brain to respond in the way we expect. Every thoughtful person aims at happiness and pursues his own goals. As individuals, our concept of happiness is different. Usually, we know but cannot find out the ambiguity in our lives. This is due to our unfulfilled dreams and wishes (because many of our desires, hopes, and goals are still not clarified).

Subconscious

Our subconscious mind is aware of our happiness, but our consciousness often cannot understand the same joy. To realize our full potential, our conscious and unconscious must work together. The subconscious is the foundation of our attitudes, emotions, and outlook on life. By using the strength of the subconscious mind, we can focus on what is important to us. Irrational fear prevents us from realizing our potential. Often, negative emotions such as fear, loss of hope, loss of faith in humans, and God will make us shrink from happiness. we can control our thoughts and free will.

Thought Control Skills

Here is an eye view of some standard mental control techniques that can help you improve your life:

Visualization: By visualizing ourselves to achieve success, we train our thinking to work towards success. It can attract positive energy. However, through positive display, seemingly impossible goals attract our good luck! Sports use this technique extensively to produce the best performance among athletes. Khalil Gibran wrote a couplet, which pointed out that no matter what you ask the universe wholeheartedly, it will give you. This reaffirms the power of positive visualization, which Rhonda Byrne also reiterated in the recent hit movie "Secrets."

Meditation: Meditation is the oldest technique for controlling thoughts. By calming views and emptying all opinions, we allow peace and calm to permeate our thoughts. Meditation quiets different thoughts, always dances in our thoughts, and gives us subconsciousness. It is scientifically proven that the alpha wave generated by the mind reaches its peak after meditation. The Alpha Wave has enriched creativity and positive thinking. Meditation enables the mind to focus on the present and only the essence.

Mirror Talk: Man is his own best friend and worst enemy. Negative self-talk becomes a self-fulfilling prophecy. Always dismissing oneself is the only way to be despised by everyone. On the other hand, if we give ourselves a positive attitude and encourage ourselves, the mind will feed and focus on the achievable goal and work towards it.

Self-Hypnosis: Self-hypnosis is like meditation, emptying all thoughts, and focusing the views on one goal. Self-hypnosis and the repetition of the only spell is a successful technique that has been used by Alcoholics Anonymous to free alcoholics from the self-destruction of alcohol.

I'm Writing Down Goals and Continuously Self-Evaluating: Writing down our goals will give them concrete forms. Always check the goals and the progress made in achieving them, allowing you to make the necessary changes. Reviewing the progress made can also help keep the goals unchanged and maintain optimism.

How to Use Psychology to Make Someone Drop in Love with You

Do you believe that love cannot be controlled? Do you think that if a person does not love you from the beginning, there is no chance? Do you believe that a person can't fall madly and deeply in love with you? If you answer "yes," then you most likely find in opportunity and destiny. Yes, many people can! Most people give the impression that love cannot be changed, and they also think that love cannot be manipulated. I think I used to feel guilty about it. But a lot of research conducted over the years proves that you can indeed control love. All of this can be done through the power of thinking. This is all about learning how to use the account correctly. You will find that love is no different from other psychological emotions you may encounter daily.

• Fear

• Pressure

• Jealousy

• Self-pity

• Anxiety

The above emotions can be controlled, and when love belongs to the category of "mental emotions," it can also be controlled. Managing love as an emotion is as easy as dealing with fear, excitement, or stress. The problem is what we are taught to believe. All this depends on "destiny." However, the actual situation is quite different with the right knowledge. There is nothing foolproof, which means this will not work 100% all the time, but you will significantly increase your chances. If you can triple the possibility of genuinely falling in love with you, why don't you try?

How We Happen to Love and The Psychology Following It

Before thinking about starting to learn how to make a person fall in love with you madly, you need to understand the psychological aspects. No, it has nothing to do with the magic potion and midnight when the moon is chanting. If you don't realize this, you and everyone else you know will store a list in your mind. On this list, there are some set conditions, and you must first meet potential love interests. Psychologists call this list "love map." If someone does not meet one or more conditions of this list, they will automatically lose their qualifications as a potential partner, and they will most likely just continue to be your friend, which is why you might fall in love with someone at some point This is the reason others will only be your "friend." Of course, everyone's list is different and unique. The items in the menu depend on you

- Values
- Belief
- Experience
- Background

• Previous relationship

This is why your friend might fall in love with a man you think is ordinary and nothing special. This person matches their own unique "love map," not yours. Counting the number of matches to see if someone fits our list is not conscious; it is done subconsciously without thinking about it. The mind can do everything by itself. It's like your accounts heartbeat tells you when you finish reading this page, even if you don't realize it consciously. This is why it is possible to fall in love with a person without knowing it. This is why emotion is such a "mysterious phenomenon". Many people regard it all as their destiny. However, this has zero to do with fate, and it has to do with your subconscious mind, which is quietly figuring out whether the person matches your list. The fact of the matter is that if you can better understand the specific criteria of the subconscious mind, then you will quickly determine why you prefer certain people over others.

How to Manipulate the Mind to Make Sure They Love You?

Here are some tried and tested methods that can help you make another person fall in love with you:

1. Meet Different Standards. All of us have this list. This list contains all the necessary measures that we expect to achieve before considering falling in love with someone. It is not confident that if a person meets these criteria, we will fall in love with them, but if they do not match, it is almost sure that we will never fall in love with them. Some examples of such criteria may include: "he must love dogs," "he must be active," "he must be educated," and so on. Please do some research before trying to make someone fall in love with you. Find all the necessary information about their background and interests-the the more you know, the better, and then try to meet their standards in this way.

2. Meet Their Unmet Needs. When looking for a new partner, they look for another person who is similar to them in many ways. They look for their advantages in one person, but the opposite of disadvantages. For example, a smart person who tends to have low self-esteem will look for a partner who is also intelligent but not with low self-esteem. They will seek the confidence to help build a better balance. If you need someone to fall in love with you and know that you have a sense of inferiority, you can effectively arouse their passion in you by showing your confidence in that person. When you play the role of a more confident person, you subconsciously send them a message telling them: "I have what you need!"

3. How Hard Did You Try? Many people often wonder if they are persevering and pursuing. If the person you are chasing is externally dependent, then the chasing is likely to succeed. External dependence means that a person relies on something or someone to make them feel better or escape from the wrong place. If a person happens into this category, they will likely seize any opportunity to establish a new relationship. In this case, the chance of making the person in question fall in love with you will be higher. When people are more vulnerable and need care, they are more likely to fall in love with you faster.

4. Use Mutual Friends. If you and your heart desire to have many friends, you can and should use it to your advantage. The main reason for this is that when a trusted source (such as a friend) backs up the content programmed with it, it can be easier to program the subconscious mind. If their friends think you are great, they are likely to agree. If their friends think you are an idiot, they are likely to accept it. This is a subtle way of brainwashing – the more your mutual friends talk to them about how beautiful you are, and the more chance you have to establish yourself in their minds.

5. Manual Wiring. The further you repeat something to someone, the more likely you are to manipulate that person into thinking about something. Why? It's effortless; constant repetition can significantly affect the subconscious acceptance of things. This, by no means, means that you have a permit to call them every ten minutes; it will only suffocate them and permanently scare them away. You can easily program their thoughts by cleverly reminding them of your presence. Stay within sight and let them see you as much as possible. It doesn't matter whether you speak very little or not. As long as you visit where they can see you, you can stand firm in their minds.

6. Compare Yourself with Positive Things. If your name is mentioned in a crowd, what is the first word that people think of? What do they think of you? Do they think "strong-willed," "happy," "confident," or negative words like "needy?" The better you position yourself in people's minds, the better people will understand you. No matter what you are (we all have negative qualities), it all has to do with how they perceive you. And you just want them to see you in a positive light.

Love at First Sight, Or Just A Myth?

At first glance, love does exist. If someone manages to meet your criteria on the subconscious list from the beginning. "Wait a minute," you said to yourself," if I have never talked to them, how can I know if they meet my standards?" It's easy. Your criteria may include things like how they stand, walk, talk, and even interact with others. This can happen if the person's behavior, appearance, or other reminds you of other people.

A typical example is if the person reminds you of someone you once loved. We usually follow a pattern and fall in love with the same type of people we loved in the past. So, if someone tells you of someone you once liked, but you don't realize they are telling you someone from the past. Then you will think that falling in love with them is "destiny."

The Secret to Controlling Others

NLP Practitioner training contains many techniques and tools that you can spend a lifetime honing your abilities. After working in NLP for many years, as a teacher and coach, I found myself gradually understanding how to combine different techniques, how to get better or faster results, and to improve my design. I realize that NLP practitioners have only recently licensed some people, and those are experienced people in the field, so I carefully selected the following techniques:

1. Develop Your Sensory Acuity: Since most of us want to get sexy body and language skills, we see that our trainers do so well and practice beautifully, thus enhancing your ability to observe what is happening, which are easily forgotten by people. However, with excellent sensory acuity, you will find that leaps and bounds will improve your work results. The more you understand your customers' changing state, calibration, and nonverbal notices, the more successful you will be.

2. Re-Focus on Your Milton Model: The Milton model has so many elements that you can improve your skills. I suggest you read the "NLP Practitioner" manual in the "Milton Model" section and see which part is worthy of attention. Practice! Maybe work 10 minutes a day, or write with a whiteboard marker on the bathroom mirror.

3. Work A Little More for Your Sub-Modes: Check out all those topics that include sub-patterns in your NLP Practitioner training. One question to ask yourself is: "Can you quickly eliminate all the different sub-models that you can ask customers to provide?" If so, how do you create your new model in a more advanced way by combining different sub-models? Get creative?

4. Put Yourself Outside Your Comfort Zone: Most of us tend to use specific parts of NLP more often than other methods. I sincerely believe in the principle of stretching, especially for more sophisticated NLP practitioners. Working with other people, working within 70% of your comfort zone, and 30% beyond your comfort zone will keep you in your best condition. 30% is where learning occurs, so if you avoid, for example, anchoring, go ahead!

5. Apply for NLP Every Day: Some of us may forget to apply NLP skills consciously to our daily lives. As NLP practitioners, we must continue to use our tools and different technologies. We will quickly become unconsciously competent, but there are usually tools that keep us at a conscious level of ability.

How NLP Improves Work Efficiency

Neural language programming describes how we perceive the external world or external influences and how to communicate this perception through the language used. In the workplace, NLP can be utilized as a tool to change individuals and ultimately significantly increase productivity. By understanding how individuals or teams interpret the world around them, you can change the way they think, speak, and behave in the world around them. NLP proposes to reverse negative attitudes and habits in the workplace so that individuals can control their reactions and feelings to future events. So, how to use NLP to improve the productivity of the team?

1. Set Goals: The easiest way to implement the NLP form in your work environment is to ensure that everyone is working towards their goals. By setting goals, you can provide direction and work assistance to the team. If employees think they are on track to achieve these firm goals, they will naturally work harder to ensure that they do. They will also automatically assume more responsibility for their roles and the work they do. This can increase personal productivity. You can also specify incentives to successfully achieve your goals to motivate employees to thrive in the work environment.

2. Improve Employee Morale: NLP is an excellent way to make employees more engaged and satisfied in the workplace.

NLP training is a valuable investment. Dedicated employees will perform better than other employees in the business – what are you doing to maintain your commitment and engagement to the market? Learning NLP technology through tailor-made training courses and coaches will enable team members to overcome obstacles in the workplace and achieve a higher level of performance. Employee morale is an ongoing factor considered by the team leader or manager. Respecting employees, listening to their ideas, and making them feel inclusive will maintain their self-esteem and confidence.

3. Better Communication: Internal communication and customer relationships are essential to producing an efficient work environment. The key to using NLP to improve communication is to make people aware of how they feel when interacting with others. NLP will help identify bad behaviors, such as body language. Body style (such as avoiding eye contact or sagging shoulders) is usually a subconscious behavior. Once the adverse reaction is recognized, the individual can strive to change and improve. As individuals become more self-aware, they also become more aware of others. Effective communication requires an understanding of the thought process of others and an understanding of oneself. See yourself the direction you want others to see you.

4. Learning and Development: NLP aims to integrate individual skills and highlight their hidden abilities. NLP releases a wealth of intellectual potential. Employees will be eager to learn and promote their professional development. This allows employees to take control of their careers and requires them to be proactive in doing so. A dynamic, dedicated, and energetic team will be full of enthusiasm and productivity. NLP helps individuals improve their job roles by hiring outstanding team members and using their behavior and professional ethics as role models adopted by others. You can have a team as strong as your most reliable employees. This will have a significant impact on productivity and give your business a competitive advantage.

5. Change Behavior: The main goal of NLP is to reverse negative behaviors and habits. According to personal explanations, their workplace has nothing to do with the actual working environment and has nothing to do with the individual. Even if everyone's working situation is the same, employees' experience is entirely different. NLP makes employees aware that the problems they encounter at work are usually internal rather than external.

What Is Hypnosis?

Hypnosis is a state similar to sleep. In this state, you are very susceptible to hints or guidance from a hypnotist. During the hypnosis process, you will enter a more focused and attentive state. A hypnotist can help you relax and become calm, which makes you more receptive to advice. Hypnosis is equivalent to daydreaming. When you daydream, you tend to block other thoughts or stimuli and focus on your daydream. During anesthesia, you also tend to concentrate entirely on what is happening immediately without being distracted by other thoughts or sounds. Hypnosis can be used to treat various diseases, conditions and discomforts. For example, suggestiveness caused by anesthesia can relieve anxiety or depression. Hypnotism can also be used to treat certain medical disorders, such as gastrointestinal diseases, skin diseases, or chronic pain, although hypnotism is not practical. Researchers also use hypnosis to obtain information about its effects on learning, memory, sensation, and perception.

To better understand how hypnosis works, let's look at an example. Imagine you bite your nails and want to get rid of this bad habit. For this, please schedule a meeting with a hypnotist. When you enter the room, the hypnotist will ask you to choose a place to sit or lie down. You tell him that you want to stop biting your nails, so the hypnotist asks you to close your eyes and imagine that you are in a place you like, such as at the beach or park. The hypnotist will guide you through some visualization operations to make you feel calm and relaxed. After relaxing, the hypnotist recommends that you no longer need to bite your nails. He asks you to visualize healthy and well-manicured nails. In your extremely calm state, this suggestion will have a more substantial impact on your thinking than other aspects. Your extraordinarily calm and relaxed state of mind makes you very imaginative. Once the suggested mental image is produced, the hypnotist will use phrases like "Now it's time to go back to the present" to trick you into opening your eyes; this way, the conversation ends.

Are You in A Trance?

There are several popular myths about hypnosis. First, some people think that the hypnotist has "power" over the person being hypnotized. This is not true. Even in a calm, hypnotic state, you can fully control what you do and imagine in the meeting; you will never be bound by anything suggested by the hypnotist. Second, some people think that hypnosis can make people unconscious. This is another myth. Throughout the hypnosis process, you can control your thoughts and hear what is happening around you. Anesthesia usually describes the hypnotized object as entirely ignorant of the surrounding environment, almost unconscious or exhibiting weird behavior involving animal noise and funny songs. Hypnosis courses are only designed to help you relax and remain calm so that you can face illness or bad habits.

The Truth About Hypnosis

Hypnosis is perhaps one of the commonly misunderstood and controversial psychotherapy methods. The myths and misunderstandings of hypnotherapy mainly stem from people's views on stage hypnotism. The fact is that stage hypnotism is essentially a dramatic performance. It has a lot in common with real clinical hypnosis, just like many Hollywood movies do in real life. But the fact is that hypnosis is a real psychological phenomenon and has valid uses in clinical practice. Under anesthesia (that is, in a hypnotic state), it seems that many people are more willing to accept useful advice than usual. Positive information given to people during hypnosis is called "post-hypnotic advice" because they are designed to take effect after the person comes out of the hypnotic effect. The advice to the hypnotist seems to be an essential part of the mechanism of the program. Although many people will not accept or respond to direct help in advance, under anesthesia, ideas seem to have entered their minds, perhaps through the "back door" of consciousness. They often sprout and take root in significant behavioral or psychological changes.

Also, not everyone is susceptible to hypnosis. Some people seem to have a trait called "hypnosis," which, like other traits, varies significantly between individuals. To be successfully hypnotized, a person must voluntarily accept the process and have a moderate level of hypnotic ability. Even profoundly hypnotized people may not benefit from hypnotherapy, and a single hypnosis session usually does not produce lasting results. Typically, a soul will have to go through a series of hypnotic procedures to reinforce the constructive suggestions that may be given. The most common clinical uses of hypnosis include: breaking bad habits, overcoming insomnia, recalling forgotten experiences, and using it as an anesthetic for pain. You can quickly test the benefits of self-hypnosis. Sit or lie down and feel comfortable in a quiet environment. Then, close your eyes, take a few deep breaths in and out slowly. This makes many people fall into the midline and a comfortable state of relaxation. In this state, say something positive to yourself (for example, "I can easily skip dessert") and imagine some social activities. Even a five-minute course is beneficial for some people.

The History of Hypnotism

When you consider hypnosis, you may think of an old black and white movie with a villain swinging a pocket watch. Do you believe that hypnosis can work? Researchers say that thinking is half the process. Due to the many myths and misunderstandings surrounding it, the topic of hypnotism has caused considerable controversy. Despite scientific research and extensive clinical applications, many people still fear hypnotism, and this hypnotism has captivated the surrounding stigma. To break down some of these ideas, we will briefly introduce you to the origin and evolution of hypnotism. Did you know that the United States has been hypnotized since the mid-1800s? You may be surprised to know that its origin can be traced back to ancient history. The famous Sanskrit book "Mandu Law" mentions many levels of hypnosis, including "sleep in a dream," "walking in sleep," and "sleep in ecstasy."

In the Middle Ages, it was commonly believed that kings and princes could heal, and they were also called "royal style." According to records, they performed magical treatments called "magnetism" or "Americanism." Paracelsus, a doctor in the 16th century, was the first to use magnets as a treatment. This treatment method was popular until the 18th century. At that time, Austrian physician Franz Mesmer discovered that he could incite without magnetism. Mesmer erroneously concluded that healing power comes from invisible forces other than magnets. Maybe you heard that someone said something fascinating?

Mesmer was the first to describe the traditional method of hypnosis, which he passed on to his followers, and their followers continued to develop the technique. Unfortunately, Frank Mesmer (Frank Mesmer) is also why we have such a mysterious view of hypnotism. He has some relatively unfamiliar and elusive methods, such as wearing a cloak and playing weird ritual music. Other doctors believe that hypnosis is not a magical power, but an instrument that opens the mind. Even so, the development of anesthesia does not have Mesmer's strange method. Throughout history, many people believed that hypnosis is a compelling psychological solution to various physical and mental illnesses. Seeing the potential of hypnotism in the medical field, some well-known doctors risked using their medical licenses. A priest named Abbe Faria began to study the effectiveness of hypnosis techniques. He proposed that it was not the magnetic field or external force that caused the magnet, but the subject's thoughts. Faria's method laid the foundation for the theoretical and clinical work of the French hypnotic psychotherapy school Nancy School (also known as the suggestion school).

The founder of the Nancy School, Ambroise-Auguste Liebault (Ambroise-Auguste Liebault) believes that hypnosis is a psychological phenomenon that ignores magnetic theory. He focused his research and hypnosis training on the correlation between falling asleep and undergo. He concluded that hypnosis is a mental state produced by suggestion. Starting from this theory, he published "Sleep and the Similar States" in 1866. His work attracted many outstanding pioneers in psychology to study at Nancy College. These include Sigmund Freud, Pierre Janet, and Hippolyte Bernheim (they went to the clinic). At the peak of hypnosis research, many doctors used hypnosis for anesthesia. In 1821, Recarmel was famous for using hypnotic trances to anesthetize patients during significant operations. Thirteen years later, British surgeon John Elliotson (who introduced the stethoscope to the UK) reported on multiple painless services performed using hypnosis.

Later more than a century of hard work, doctors and researchers have finally been able to remove the Mesmer stains left by hypnosis practice and reveal it as a useful clinical technique. At the end of the 19th century, hospitals and medical universities explored anesthesia and research and applied anesthesia to many medical abnormalities. Although there are many predecessors in his field, Scottish ophthalmologist James Braid is known as the "father of modern hypnotism." He was the first personality to coin the term "neural hypnosis." This term was reduced to hypnotism in 1841. In the next century, the use of hypnotism surged and was incorporated into medical practice for rapid treatment after World War I and World War II. After hundreds of years of development and documentation, modern technology has helped reveal the truth. By using brain imaging, doctors and researchers can see that hypnosis is its state. This is not a, nor is it a vacancy. On the contrary, it is a real state of mind, and the theme is easy to change and accept new ideas, our very conscious state has been trained to be something that can be stopped.

Hypnosis Techniques

In the first step of hypnosis, hypnosis is a process used by hypnotists to bring clients into a state of being more receptive to suggestions (called daze). There are many types of induction:

Relaxation Techniques: Why should the therapist "make yourself comfortable" and provide a relaxing leather sofa to lie down on? This is more than ordinary courtesy. Relaxation is a standard method used by therapists and a hypnotic technique for beginners. If the client relaxes, they may fall into a deep sleep and be open-minded. They are more inclined to talk to you and are willing to accept indirect suggestions. Here are some common ways to relax:

- Make yourself comfortable
- Lie down
- Reciprocal breathing control
- Relax and tense muscles
- Speak in a soft tone

Handshake Technique: The father of hypnotherapy, Milton Erickson (Milton Erickson), is known for using handshake techniques to induce hypnosis. Handshake is the usual common way of greeting in our society. The handshake technique disrupted this daily social norm and shocked the subconscious. Hypnotists usually do not shake hands, but instead interrupt the established patterns in our minds by grabbing the wrist or pulling the object forward and unbalance the body. With the termination of the model, the subconscious suddenly accepted the suggestion.

Eyeball Cue: The brain has two areas: the right side manages the more "creative" and conscious aspects, while the left side controls the "practical" and subconscious. In any conversation, we seek feedback from the audience to understand how they react to our statement. Watch the subject's eyes. Do they look to the right, into the consciousness, or to the left into the subconscious? Are they fixed to an object in the room? If they are visiting the subconscious mind, it can be suggested that they are not consciously aware of it.

Advanced Technique: Eye Contact

Reading listeners' eye movements are a daily use case. Yet, did you know that, as a speaker, you can also induce hypnosis to the audience through eye movements? This new technology was developed and tested by Stephen Brooks.

Visualization: Visualization can be used to attract people or to make suggestions. For example, ask your subjects to recall a room they are very familiar with. Imagine every detail in the room: the floor, the shape of the window, the painting on the wall, the smell, the light. Then, move to a place they are not familiar with. When they try to recall the exact details, they open up to accept suggestions.

Advanced Tip: Use visualization to remember positive memories, associate them with beneficial behaviors, or change people's perceptions of negative images.

- Positive images and experiences (wedding, children, birthday, graduation)
- Discard poor images (maybe throw them in the trash can)

Arm "Levitation" Technology: With this classic Erickson technology, customers first have to close their eyes. They were required to pay attention to the difference in sensation between their arms. The hypnotherapist advises on how each department feels. For example, they may say that the gun feels heavy or light, hot or cold. The client enters a state and may physically lift the armor, and they simply believed that they raised their arms. Either way, induction is successful.

Sudden Shock/Regression: Proceed with caution! Similar to the handshake technique, subjects will fall into a deep sleep when they find themselves shocked. I never advocate causing any physical pain to a topic, but Eriksson has proven this by stepping on women's feet and making suggestions. The milder version is the "decline of trust" in team-building activities you may have heard of or participated in. The feeling of retreat shook the entire system and opened up the mind for suggestions. However, it must be ensured that they will not abandon the subject.

Fixed Eyes: Have you ever found yourself "partitioning" and staring at an unusual object in the room while talking? Do you miss their words completely? You may have been hypnotized. Any focused purpose can be used to induce a trance. The most famous examples are the "electric pendulum" or "swing pocket watch," although both objects are now associated with hockey stage hypnosis. Because of the reputation of these objects, you are more likely to fail and encounter resistance. However, there are two secrets behind fixed eyeballs. First, the purpose makes the conscious thought occupy, and makes the subconscious open the suggestion. Secondly, when you look at or move back and forth, your eyes will feel physical fatigue. Example: Try to look up at the ceiling for a few minutes (do not bend your neck). The eyes are naturally tired and begin to close.

Body Scan: A popular method of self-hypnosis. Start from the top of the body with your eyes closed, and slowly scan down from head to toe. Pay attention to every sensation-your breathing that expands your chest, the back of your chair is on your body, the pain in your elbow, each finger sticks out, and your foot is on the ground. Repeat the process from bottom to top. Continue to scan up and down until you enter.

Advanced Tip: Body scanning can be used in combination with other hypnosis-inducing techniques (such as countdown breathing and relaxation) to improve the effect.

Countdown Breath: You may have heard that meditation controls breathing, but it can also be a natural form of hypnosis. It works as follows:

- Close your eyes, and remain upright on the chair with your arms on your legs.
- Breathe deeply through your nose, then breathe through your mouth.
- Use slow controlled breathing, counting down from 100.
- Each exhalation is counted as an interval.
- In the end, please continue to practice decreasing from higher numbers.

Hypnosis Advice: The recommendation is the desired behavior to be performed by the client. The post-hypnotic proposal is made after the hypnotized person enters into trance, and in this state, they are more susceptible to influence. There are two suggested schools of thought.

Indirect Suggestion: Eriksson is a proponent of indirect advice. It is a love of certified hypnotherapists because it puts the control in the hands of the subject, not autocratic-respecting patient boundaries and clinical ethics. Also, it has proven to be more effective against resistance or suspicion. Rather than "commanding" an object to relax (direct suggestion), it is better to say: "You may want to close your eyes when you are comfortable."

Direct Suggestion: In conversational hypnosis, straightforward suggestions are explicit commands to perform specific actions. Although powerful, it can sometimes be seen as unethical because, as an authority (doctor or hypnotist), you control the customer. The client does not constrain the decision to change behavior using this method. The Stanford Prison Experiment is a notorious example of using authority, obedience, and direct advice to manipulate subjects.

Here are some excellent direct suggestions:

- "You will go to sleep."
- "You will stop smoking."
- "You will lose weight."

Intonation: Voice tone is especially useful when making suggestions. This can be doubled with other techniques (such as relaxation)."You might want to relax. "In the example above, the word "slack" is stretched gently. Instead, you can make direct suggestions out loud. "You will stop smoking!" Another perfect voice pair is obfuscation. The therapist can improve the tone of the voice, from whispering to shouting, speaking in a different accent, or slurring to confuse the subject.

Hypnosis Trigger: There are many forms of hypnotic triggers. The trigger reminds the subconscious mind of a desired action or sensation, which is implied under hypnosis. Here are some examples:

- Open one's eyes

- Bells
- Snap
- Clap
- Standing or sitting down
- Open the door

Here are how hypnotic triggers can be applied to agoraphobia: "When you open a door, you may see your loving family on the other side."

Non-Verbal Communication: Hypnotists are experts in nonverbal communication-from reading a client's body language to conveying your nonverbal advice. When the customer may consciously say one thing, the subconscious mind will tell a completely different story. Here are some examples of how the subconscious mind affects body language:

- Facial expression
- Body posture
- Intonation
- Pacing
- Eye movement
- Arms crossed
- Head nod
- Cover face

Cold Reading: You may have seen psychologists, media, stage hypnotists, or psychologists doing "cold reading" on TV for entertainment purposes. Although it is usually impossible to use it directly with customers, you can use cold reading at parties or social events. This is how cold reading works. For example, if the case is not smiling, the hypnotist may ask:

H: "Are you sad?" - First, request a general or vague question from observation.

S: "Yes" - If they answered "No," please reset and ask another vague question.

H: "Has anyone left you?" - Go deeper and ask more specific questions. This could be a relationship, and it could be a pet or family member.

S: "Yes! How do you know my cat is fluffy and dead?"

Warm Reading: Through enthusiastic reading, you can make a statement that applies to anyone: "You will be happy when your friends surround you."

Popular Reading: The most challenging type, because you need to know this person first. Suppose their family members contacted you and told you that the person was involved in a traumatic event. When you meet them, you may focus on using "attribution" techniques because you have prior knowledge of past events.

Swish Model: Sub-modes can be used in "swing mode," which is a neural language programming technique used to associate or separate customers from certain behaviors. The five senses are considered forms (taste, smell, sight, touch, and hearing).

Sub-modality is a subset of these feelings. Here are some examples of sub-patterns:

- Bright or dim?
- Big or small?
- Color or black and white?
- Is it loud or small?

The swish mode starts with visualization. Once the client is in trouble, the hypnotist will determine one or two sub-modes. Unwanted movements are prominent in the foreground, concentrated and bright, while the desired effect can be seen as small and dark. When you say "Swish" (the name of the method), the desired image quickly becomes bright and essential in the customer's mind.

Misleading: From politics to entertainment, we see that the real world sometimes uses misleading every day. The prefix means an error, and "direction" is appended to it, guiding the viewer in the wrong direction. There are two types of misleading, one is textual errors, and the other is mental errors. The first simple demonstration is that the magician uses his left hand to wave a magic wand, and then his right hand distracts people. When the audience was misled, the magician sneaked a card on his sleeve, giving the illusion that it "disappeared." Misleading can also be visualized: "When you become anxious, imagine you are relaxing on the beach." Here, an anxiety sufferer is misled into his image on the beach. The hypnotist guides them from unpleasant images to pleasant ones.

Reframe: Reframe is usually a metaphor that allows you to change the perception of experience in customers' minds. For example, assume you have a client who wants to lose weight. They stay in it all day to play video games. You can ask them to describe the process of "upgrading" a character in a video game-what they do, how long it takes, and how strong the character is in the beginning. Then, by comparing it with video games, they "reframed" their weight loss process. "Losing weight is like raising the level of a character in a video game. You start slowly and train every day. At first, you don't see much difference, but as time goes by, your "character" becomes more durable and reliable."

Lead to Regression: First, the customer enters a deep trance state where they can experience the authenticity of the event (also known as sleepwalking). The therapist uses the visualization function to create an "impact bridge," where the client can experience it again. After determining the cause, the hypnotherapist can make recommendations and reformulate the situation.

The Pace in The Future: The opposite of regression is when the subject is asked to visualize itself and take appropriate actions and behaviors. You are looking forward to events full of positive emotions, not looking back at potential adverse events in the past. "Imagine that your speech is finished, and the crowd is cheering. You will feel satisfied and relieved."

Anchored: When we record memories, all senses and emotions are related. These are the "anchors" in your mind. Perhaps the client has anchored smoking behavior with rest, eating, making love, chatting with friends, and other pleasant feelings. The hypnotist can suggest a new anchor and get a more positive response.

Betty Erickson's 3-2-1 Technique: Betty Erickson is the wife of Milton Erickson. She developed a method of self-hypnosis called the 3-2-1 technique. The procedure starts with opening your eyes. You will notice three things you can see, hear, and feel in the room. For example, you might see paintings, tables, and clocks on the walls. You may listen to the birds outside the window, the hum of the refrigerator, and the clock's ticking. You may feel the back of the chair, your feet on the floor, and the warmth of the sun. Repeat this process, focusing on two items per sensation, and then one thing (hence the name 3-2-1). Then, you close your eyes and visualize three objects from each of your senses on your head. Once again, you count down. After reaching the last item, you will be in.

Incrementalism: Making small changes is a stepping stone to significant changes. For example, if a buyer is trying to lose weight, the daily aerobic exercise may be too much. Instead, you can suggest that they start in smaller increments: go up a flight of stairs, then jump into the elevator as usual. Next week, two flights of stairs. Ultimately, they will achieve higher goals and overall, more desirable behavior. The promise is small, and it is impossible to fail. You may stay for more than 5 minutes, thus adding a month and days.

Parts Therapy: In theory, all behaviors are positive to some extent. The subconscious mind can use affirmative action to prove negative behavior. Acrophobia may not leave home because the unconscious purpose is to protect the body from outside harm. Smokers may harm their bodies to seek pleasant conversations with other smokers outside. The mind is made up of various sections. Through local therapy, the hypnotherapist communicates with the behavioral part to better understand why it is required. Then, they will interact creatively with thinking to come up with another solution. Taking smokers as an example, there may be another way to meet the needs of a social interaction-a book club, a bowling ball. Then, the therapist uses future rhythm to enhance positive behavior.

Metaphor: Metaphors are therapeutic and unforgettable. Eriksson likes to use metaphors in his books and teachings. Here are some classic analogies:

- Your body is a car, and give it the right fuel, it will perform well. If you neglect maintenance and inject the wrong fuel into it, it will be damaged.

- Your thoughts are like a river flowing. You can stand on the river bank and watch it go by, or you can try to swim against the current.
- You are a mountain-strong, durable, and high.

Hypnotic Binding: Hypnotic binding is a favorite among parents and presents the "illusion" of choice through one or more questions. This is an example: "Do you require to brush your teeth or take a bath?" Advanced tip: Using double binding provides two options for the same desired behavior: "Do you want to go to bed in 10 or 20 minutes?" Either way, the child is performing the required go to bed action.

Hypnotic Logic: Under trance, the client explains the sentence very truthfully. If you ask customers, "can you sit up" they will answer "yes." We call this a kind of hypnotic logic. You can use hypnotic logic and similar suggestions: "Because of success, you can lose weight." Although success does not necessarily mean that you can lose weight, it is a measure to be taken.

Affirmation and Positive Thinking: Affirm the positive thoughts. For clients with deformities, you may ask them to repeat the "I am beautiful" daze.

Reconnect: The memory disappears with time. It may be a good thing for people experiencing negative experiences, positive experiences will gradually go. Just like memory, the ability can also be forgotten. Phobias may forget that once they could go outdoors. As a hypnotherapist, you can help bring back these positive memories and skills through rehearsals and visualizations with clients.

Is Hypnosis Mind Control?

Hypnosis is not "brain control" because it is not a mandatory process. The typical "tramp" associates anesthesia with mental control because hypnosis is usually depicted in movies. No wonder so many people worry about hypnosis! Hypnosis induction itself is a cooperation between the hypnotist/coach and the subject/volunteer. In other words, hypnosis is a collaborative process. In a hypnotic performance stage, the hypnotic performer seems to be able to make the hypnotized volunteer do anything. Of course, this audience perception increases the entertainment value of the performance and makes hypnosis seem mysterious. The experience of hypnotized volunteers on stage is more like a relaxed daydream state. They feel good, and they are willing to experience hypnosis in a particular range voluntarily. What are these boundaries? Before recruiting volunteers, the stage hypnotist will give a short speech to explain the myths and misunderstandings of hypnotism. This pre-chat sets the limits of the program. The opening remarks of the stage hypnotist created an "implied contract" for the volunteers during the hypnotic performance. Usually, this means that the volunteer will experience strange and unusual hypnosis, but will not cross the moral boundaries. If the stage hypnotist violates the volunteer's implicit contract, they will usually jump out of the state, feeling like: "Hey, I didn't sign up?!" They can choose to leave the stage directly.

How to Hypnotize with Eyes

Hypnosis seems impressive; in fact, there is a lot of practice and science behind hypnotizing someone. One of the several effective ways to hypnotize someone is to enter the mind with the eyes. However, only use this practice before the people who conquer them, then hypnotize them and always use your abilities in a responsible way.

Do Eye Exercises

Try to Maintain Eye Contact for A Long Time Without Blinking. Look in the mirror and see how long you can maintain eye contact without blinking.

- You can also test your abilities in staring matches with others.
- Full control of your eye movements will help you maintain steady eye contact with others during hypnosis.

Practice the Ability to Focus on The Eyes. To do this, first look at the close objects (such as pens or pencils), and then look at the distant objects in the room.

- Bring the pencil close to your face. Focus on the pen.

- Move from focusing on the pencil to more distant objects, such as pictures on the wall or door handles.
- Return to focus on the pen. Then focus on distant objects. Continue to practice this to improve focus flexibility.

Increase Your Awareness of Peripheral Devices. This is your capacity to see objects and movements on both sides without turning your head. To improve this feature, do the following:

- Sit in a busy scene outside on the sidewalk. Or sit in the port of a TV or computer screen that is playing lively scenes.
- Try to look at the active stage, turning your head to the side. Then turn your head and look to the other side. Try to see as many scenes as possible from both sides.
- Make sure you practice from left to right.

Hypnotize with Eyes

Ask for Permission. Make sure they say "yes" by asking them: "Can I hypnotize?"

- It is best to practice hypnotism with your trusted friends or relatives because they are more willing to be hypnotized.
- This person must be someone willing to participate. If they resist or don't require to be hypnotized, then hypnosis may not work.

Let the Person Sit in A Comfortable Upright Position.
Don't let them stand because they may become very relaxed
during hypnosis, and if they rise, they will fall. Tell the body to
focus on a spot under the right eye. Instruct them not to look
away when talking to them.

I Was Staring at Them Without Blinking. Start counting
from 5 to 1 with a soft, deep voice. As you wish, please tell them:

- "Your eyelids are getting heavier."
- "Your eyelids are getting heavier and heavier, like a heavyweight pulling them down."
- "Soon, your eyelids will become so heavy that they will close."
- "The more you open your eyes, the heavier they become, the more likely they are to become loose, tied, and locked up."
- Count from 5 to 1, repeat these phrases several times.

Tell This Person That You Are Going to Touch Their Shoulders, And They Will Become MP-Ready. Before
contacting them, you must tell the person what will happen.
This will make them determined to understand that you will give
them an order, and they will respond by performing what you
tell them.

- Tell the other person: "When I touch your shoulders, you will become slack, lithe and heavy. Are you ready?"

Touch People's Shoulders and Tell Them It's Time to Relax. If the person falls or leans back on the chair, don't panic. This shows that they have completely relaxed and are now under hypnosis.

Make Sure That The Person Is Now Under Hypnosis. People must be aware that they are relaxed due to anesthesia or hypnosis.

- It is also essential to ensure personal safety and health. Please rest assured that they will continue to trust you and listen to your orders.

Tell the Person That Their Best Arm Should Now Be Loose and Dense. Inform them that they should feel pleasant and relaxed. Then, touch their arms to trigger their response.

- Raise their arms to confirm that it is now relaxed. Put back their arms in place.

- This confirms that the person is now in the state. It also shows that they are prepared to listen to your voice and your commands.

Set Them to Listen Only to Your Voice. Count down from 5 to 1. Tell them that when you enter "one," they will only listen to you.

- Press your fingers on "one" to focus them on the voice. Tell them to let your call relax them more deeply. Then, instruct them to listen to every word you say, only to every word you say.

- Instruct them only to follow your terms correctly, and there is no other voice around.

Test Their Hypnotic State. Now that you have hypnotized the person, you can test your abilities by having them touch their nose or ears. You can also put them to move their arms or legs as ordered.

- Remember, hypnotics must be used with caution responsibly. This person trusts you, so don't abuse it by embarrassing or hurting them under hypnosis.

Understanding Hypnosis

One Piece: Don't confuse hypnosis with falling asleep or coma. Hypnosis is a highly concentrated state of mind that allows you to learn more about suggestions and accept them more easily.

- It is essential to remember that a hypnotic state will not lose control or be under the spell of a hypnotist. Instead, the person will be more willing to accept advice and guidance.

- Usually, we are in a state of hypnosis or trance. Think about when you partition during class or get lost in your daydream. When you are addicted to movies or TV shows, you lose your awareness of the people around you. These are all instances in a state.

Pay Attention to The Benefits of Hypnosis. Hypnosis is a fun party trick and a way to get your best friend to participate in a chicken dance. Hypnosis has been shown to help people overcome insomnia, smoking, overeating, and other diseases.

Remember, Hypnosis Is Any Other Trained Skill. There is currently no hypnotic state regulation. However, hypnotherapists can be certified in basic or advanced courses in hypnosis and hypnotherapy. However, this is a self-regulating profession.

- Certification courses cover issues such as professional ethics and necessary hypnotic skills.
- Seek a certified hypnotherapist for more information about the health benefits of hypnosis.

How to Hypnotize Yourself

- Lie down comfortably and fix your eyes to a certain point on the ceiling. It should be slightly behind you, causing your eyes to fatigue when you look at it.
- Take a deep breath.
- Repeat "sleep" loudly or mentally when you inhale, and repeat "deep sleep" when exhaled. Do this for some minutes until you start to become drowsy.
- It is recommended to close your eyes.
- Deepen the hypnotic state by counting. "When I count to three, I will go deeper into a deep hypnotic state; I

will rely on three more easily." Repeat this version several times to yourself.

- Count to three, and repeat the command every time: "One becomes more relaxed. Two deeper relaxations and three are in a relaxed state, in a hypnotic state."

- Once hypnotized, you can use this counting method to program yourself to perform various operations, including bringing these commands into everyday life a longer count can help. Here are some examples:

- "At ten o'clock, my right arm will feel weightless and lift on its own. One is getting lighter."

- "At the age of ten, I will love my family and friends even more."

- "When I count to ten, I will continue caring for my family and friends."

- "Based on ten people, I will completely forgive my friends."

- "Starting from the tenth, I will no longer have headaches."

Regular hypnosis requires practice. You can test the depth of trance through physical tests such as weightless arms. Other tests include heavy eyelids and an uncontrollable urge to swallow, making the limbs feel heavier or tingling. If you cannot induce any of these effects, please be patient. You may need to spend more time in the initial "sleep/deeper sleep" phase and extend the count for each command. Another key to going more profound is the use of visual images. Together with counting, "seeing" oneself walk downstairs every time you count, take the elevator or take the escalator.

Can Improve Daily Useful Tasks Through Hypnosis

You can use the quick hypnosis course before starting the job. These include:

- Enhance your focus before doing time-consuming tasks such as coding or spreadsheets
- Build confidence before essential meetings
- Reduce anxiety before public speaking
- Strengthen the will to exercise every day
- Help yourself stick to a tricky diet
- Program to stay calm just in case you have a dispute
- Tolerate people and yourself
- Reduce road anger

Use Hypnosis to Improve Meditation

Once you enter the hypnotic state, you can begin meditation. Your meditation will be sincere and peaceful, and you will feel the effects of this meditation The understanding of hypnosis has come a long way. Ever since Hollywood portrayed the bearded man in the top hat, the pocket watch's swing has attracted people's attention. Few people realize how a powerful tool hypnosis is or how to use it to stimulate profound changes in people's emotions, thoughts and habits. One of the most comfortable and most affordable ways to start enjoying the benefits of hypnosis is to practice self-hypnosis: This means getting into a deeper state of mind and keeping specific goals in mind. Self-hypnosis is more relaxed than you think-no special skills, pocket watches, or funny beards are required.

Step 1: Clear Goals: Do you want to overcome limiting beliefs? Bad habits, like smoking or emotional eating? Or are you trying to cure a particular disease? Hypnosis works best when each link focuses on only one central goal-so figure it out first.

Step 2: Get Comfort: Put on the most comfortable clothes and move to a quiet room, away from loud offspring, spouses, pets, or electronics. You can choose to sit or lie down, but if you fall asleep quickly, you may want to stay seated. Make sure not to cross your legs or sit on any part of your body, as this may be distracting.

Step 3: Enter A More Inward State of Mind: First, focus your eyes on a corner of the front wall. Feel the eyelids heavier and then begin to close slowly. Next, concentrate on breathing and your physical and mental stress. Count down from 5 to 0 and imagine yourself as relaxing more deeply. Just like meditation, don't fight with distracting thoughts that will inevitably disturb you-just let them pass naturally.

Step 4: Re-Plan Your Thinking: When in a deeper state, two main hypnotic tools can be used:

1. Visualization: Visualize the vivid scenes where you have achieved your goals. For example, if you want to be more confident, you can imagine the applause when you speak on stage. Focus on the image emotions created with your mind; this will increase your experience and results.

2. Affirmation: Make a positive statement as if you have achieved your goal: "My life and body have always been in the best condition!" Or, "I don't smoke anymore, and I will be happier without cigarettes." If you like, you can write them down in advance. Continue for a few minutes of visualization and confirmation. Don't worry about being distracted or having difficulty imagining a particular situation- when giving you these suggestions, just let the flow go.

Step 5: Self-Cancel Hypnosis: Start counting from one to five, visualize yourself, and become more alert every time you score. When you count to five, slowly open your eyes, shake your fingers and toes, and roll your shoulders. Take a deep breath, don't worry if you're a little tired, you will be back to normal in a minute or two.

Tip: For best results, try hypnosis several days a week. Through practice, you will find yourself immersed in deeper and deeper relaxation, and each lesson can bring a smoother and more fruitful experience. Almost immediately.

Hypnotize Yourself for Success

You can gain your inner personal strength through hypnosis and thus achieve success. You can plan a successful life for yourself. Everyone has inherent potential, but many of us have lost the combination of storing their inherent personal power in the vault. Hypnosis can help you retrieve combinations to open the file library and unleash your potential. Speaking, you can hypnotize yourself to succeed for a lifetime. The concept of hypnotic success is not as reminiscent as it seems. You will not walk around in the hypnotic fog, will not be controlled by some invisible forces, will not be aware of yourself and the world around you. This common misunderstanding of hypnosis is what film studios, voodoo specialty shops, and self-proclaimed witches have made millions of dollars from. The truth of hypnosis is this: through hypnosis, you can have an enlightened feeling about yourself and the world in your life.

Not only can you view black and white images, but you can also see bursts of color and other options that you can't see due to narrow thinking. This enhanced self-awareness will enable you to find and release the personal power inherent in success. You don't need to know hypnosis to use some hypnotic techniques to make yourself and your life more successful. The theme of hypnosis is fascinating and has a long history of use. If you want to study this exciting theme further, you can go back to the early 1900s. You can use some do-it-yourself hypnosis techniques to program your mind and body for success. These methods require only a small amount of reading and repeated practice to use until you tap them and get the most benefit from using them.

Although hypnosis has a long history and uses in our society, some people call hypnosis the new era. The term "new age" can keep some people out. They chose nothing to do with everything created in the modern era. This is mainly due to the fear of the social stigma attached to practices that are often widely misunderstood. Unfortunately, due to this wrong interpretation and wrong hypnotic label, people cannot experience hypnosis. Let you open up to think and feel in a variety of different and more effective ways, and realize your power to achieve your life goals, which will not make you feel embarrassed. This is an investment in you and the success you want in life. Hypnosis is just a more valuable tool that can help you get more of what you want.

There are many myths about hypnosis, and you might think that anesthesia is nothing more than scented candles, flutes, and spiritual chanting. These things are beneficial for setting the mood or atmosphere and can even be used as a relaxation strategy or a way to clear your mind in preparation for hypnosis, but these are not the techniques you use to hypnotize successfully. To succeed in trance, you will focus on the precise goals you set. By focusing your mind and body on your goals and the steps you need to take to reach them, you are preparing for success. A firm focus can help you make the most of your power and achieve your success. You can find many high-quality reference materials to show you how to hypnotize successfully through books, DVDs, and the Internet. Hypnosis and NLP (Neuro-Language Programming) trainers are great resources to provide you with an introduction to self-hypnosis and expert guidance on using self-hypnosis techniques for more success.

Can Hypnosis Make You Smarter?

The way hypnosis is described in daily life reduces it to a party trick. But it doesn't stop there. I want to know that all of us can improve our intelligence, so I want to learn more about hypnosis. Can hypnosis make you smarter? Yes, it can. Evidence shows that studying under anesthesia, concentration, and imagination is enhanced. By entering a deeper level of subconsciousness, you can improve your learning ability and your intelligence. Sounds neat, doesn't it? Read on to learn more about hypnosis and its connection with making you smarter, how it works, and what hypnosis is usually used for. Now, I have never been hypnotized in the traditional sense, at least not yet.

Can Hypnosis Make You Smarter?

There is no doubt that hypnosis is a hotly debated topic. You can find opinions on all aspects of the problem. You either think that anesthesia is useful or you think it is ridiculous. Do you believe this is a fun party game for magicians, or support it as a recognized aid in the medical field? Sometimes people are hypnotized. Sometimes people cannot be hypnotized. The truth is that there is no definite answer to the effectiveness of hypnosis. That being said, those who work and believe in hypnosis will tell you that it can make you smarter.

Hypnosis and The Subconsciousness

It is important because the subconscious mind is where all content is stored and where information is extracted. It can save your memory, including everything you learn. Hypnosis has shown promise to reduce stress and improve concentration by eliminating everything unnecessary in the task. With better focus and concentration, you can learn new skills, such as math, languages, and even musical instruments. Research has been conducted on children who do not understand a particular subject. When they received hypnotherapy, they finally showed an excellent understanding of the same problems they had never mastered before. Sometimes, even more than the smartest peers. This will not make you a super genius overnight. But you already know. However, if you want to improve your score in a particular subject or adopt an entirely new skill, then hypnosis can help you. Seeing as so many people believe in it; there is no loss in trying it.

How Does Hypnosis Work on Earth?

No one knows how hypnosis works. There are several ideas from changing how the two halves of the brain interact with increasing blood flow to the brain. There is no accepted reason hypnosis can do this. The most popular theories are related to consciousness and subconsciousness. Your conscious or clear mind is always yours to deal with. These are your progressive ideas. This is what makes you question and stress the smallest things. It is Thomas who doubts your instincts in his mind. Your mindful is usually your worst enemy. Your subconscious mind is where items are stored. It is located deep in the conscious brain, and only appears when you are very relaxed or sleeping. Or, in this example, when you enter a state of hypnosis. There is no boundary to how much information the subconscious mind can contain, making it an ideal access point for learning new things. If you enter a state of hypnosis, you will work directly with your subconscious mind. This means that all parts of your conscious mind that might prevent you from learning or retaining information are put aside, thus opening up huge potential. It eliminates any confidence issues and all usual distracting factors, helping you focus on the task at hand. When you exclude the environment, imagine what you can accomplish. When you try to learn, you don't have to worry about those little troubles. Instead, your idea is to focus 100% on obtaining this specific information so that it can be recalled later. It is so refreshing to think you can relax and study at the same time!

Are You Hypnotized?

Many people are doing hypnosis. They range from birthday party sorcerers to certified medical professionals. However, is it possible for you to hypnotize yourself? Believe it or not – yes! You may even hypnotize yourself without knowing it. Technically speaking, the time for a few minutes to lose yourself is the same as hypnosis. Staring at a fire or driving a long distance can fascinate you, which may be better than the guy with the pocket watch TV. In addition to occasional hypnosis, there are some ways to practice real things without professional help. Perhaps you don't have the time or funds to spend an afternoon hypnotizing. Maybe you are not sure if you believe it. You can use pre-recorded hypnotic tracks or confirmations to guide yourself into a similar state. If you are not familiar with the whole hypnosis method, it is best to take the pre-recorded route. Listening to others is an excellent way to get out of touch with reality. Not everyone can concentrate on themselves. There are plenty of guided hypnosis options online. You can find records that need to be paid for free. Usually, you can pay with this kind of thing. You should also know that certified hypnotherapists will not create these self-directed hypnotics. If you want to make real transactions at home, it is worth studying. You should find yourself created by someone who knows what you are doing.

What's the Use of Hypnosis?

Hypnotism has been used for decades to recover from many different diseases, many of which are related to the mind. It is especially useful for illnesses exacerbated by stress such as anxiety, high blood pressure, and tension headaches. From public speaking to dental surgery, its use has made people carefree.

Other conditions of hypnotherapy:

- Childbirth
- Chronic pain
- Sleep disorder
- Obsessive-compulsive disorder
- Phobia
- Addiction
- Depression
- Weight loss

Hypnosis is considered an effective treatment method used by psychologists, doctors, dentists, and even chiropractors. Its public reputation may be far from making it look legitimate. The more research conducted, over 14,000 items, and still increasing, the more we understand the mystery of hypnosis and its real impact on the brain.

Hypnosis Unlocks the Mind

No one fully understands the mystery of hypnosis. Although significant steps are being taken every day to solve this problem, this is still one of the things that no one seems to be able to agree on in one way or another. Hypnosis shows excellent promise in the fields of learning and intelligence. It opens up your brain and helps you access and retain information more deeply. When you need to recall what you have learned, everything is overflowing, and you can put it on paper.

How to Hypnotize People Without Knowing It?

There are many hypnotism methods, but the common question is "how to hypnotize someone without knowing it. " If you have practiced and are determined to achieve this goal, it is easy to hypnotize people without knowing it. Studies have shown that everyone enters a hypnotic state many times a day, mainly when working repeatedly. So, if you need to know how to hypnotize someone without knowing, you can check the following and practice and implement it.

Grab Notifications from Your Subject: How to hypnotize someone without knowing someone, "The first thing is to find topics and attract their attention. Focus them on your face and words so you can captivate them. There is a lot of wrong information about hypnotism, especially those that indicate that a person needs to relax. The person you want to hypnotize needs to focus on what you are telling them, and their happiness or unhappiness, frustration or satisfaction does not matter. If you make sure to focus on what you are talking about and forget about your surroundings, it will help.

Praise Your Subject: Each of us likes to be respected. Whenever we get compliments, we feel so happy that we tend to forget everything that is happening around us. Once someone compliments us, we will be glad to hear everything he wants to say. Therefore, pure praise will win your subject's confidence and help you increase your focus.

Nod When You Blurt Out the Command: When you order the subject, you also start to nod. Nodding will have a similar effect on your questions, and they will follow you. They will nod their heads and track your orders. That's it, and you have successfully hypnotized your first subject. Therefore, you now know how to hypnotize someone. If you follow the five steps above, hypnotizing someone without knowing it is secure. And don't forget that practice is essential. Before trying someone, you want to practice with friends or family.

Health Benefits of Hypnosis

Hypnosis is often described as a control strategy, making people commit crimes or fall in love. Hypnotists are usually considered weird magicians; when they hear the word "horse," they put people on stage and make them neighbors. Hypnosis appears in the media and may seem unusual, but hypnosis has more factors than entertainment. Hypnosis can benefit your health and well-being. "In healthcare, hypnosis can be psychotherapy that can help you experience changes in feelings, perceptions, thoughts, or behavior. It is done in a clinical setting and is performed by a trained, licensed healthcare professional Personnel (such as psychologists or physicians)," said Dr. Alison T. Grant, physician of Penn Family and Internal Medicine Cherry Hill. Hypnosis usually includes recommendations for relaxation, calmness, and overall health. These recommendations may continue throughout treatment, but can sometimes be reactivated by the patient later. The conventional method involves instructions to consider pleasant experiences or verbal cues to get you into a like state. Hypnotherapy is a kind of therapy that uses hypnosis as a standalone or complementary therapy-can that benefits your health in many ways. Hypnosis can help you solve the following six common health problems:

Trouble Sleeping, Insomnia, And Sleepwalking

If you sleepwalk or struggle with falling asleep, hypnosis may be a useful tool. If you have insomnia, hypnosis can relax you enough to make it easier for you to fall asleep. If you are a sleepwalker, hypnotism can also train you to get up and help you avoid sleepwalking when you feel your foot on the floor. And if you just want to sleep better, hypnotism can also help you. Learning self- techniques can increase your sleep time and deep sleep time. This is a kind of sleep that you need to wake up and feel refreshed. Its working principle is: verbal cues make you in a like state, similar to how you feel when you are addicted to books or movies without exploring what is happening around you. After hypnosis, even during hypnosis, you will fall asleep.

Anxiety

Relaxation techniques, including hypnosis, can sometimes relieve anxiety. Hypnosis is often more useful for people who are worried about chronic health conditions (such as heart disease) rather than a generalized anxiety disorder. If you suffer from phobias, then hypnotism may also help.

How It Works: Hypnosis helps anxiety by encouraging your body to activate its natural relaxation response by using phrases or nonverbal cues, breathing slowly, lowering blood pressure, and instilling overall well-being.

Irritable Bowel Syndrome (IBS) Symptoms

Clinical research has always supported the effectiveness of hypnosis for IBS. IBS is abdominal pain caused by the intestines. Hypnosis can help improve symptoms such as constipation, diarrhea, and bloating. Dr. Grant explained: "IBS sometimes causes secondary symptoms like nausea, fatigue, backache, and urinary problems. Hypnosis has also been shown to help them."

How It Works: Hypnosis will guide you to gradually relax, providing soothing images and sensations to combat symptoms.

Chronic Pain

Hypnosis can relieve pain, such as migraine or tension headache after surgery. It can also help relieve chronic pain. Patients with anxiety related to diseases such as arthritis, cancer, sickle cell disease, and fibromyalgia, as well as those with lower back pain, may find relief from hypnosis.

How It Works: Hypnosis can help you cope with pain and enhance self-control of anxiety. Also, research shows that hypnosis can do this effectively for a long time.

Quit Smoking

"It is not obvious to give up cigarettes. There are many ways to help you quit smoking, such as nicotine patches or prescription drugs. Although this study has not been conducted, many people find that hypnosis can help them quit smoking." Dr. Grant explained. If you work one-on-one with a hypnotherapist, hypnotherapy can help quit smoking and the hypnotherapist can customize the hypnotic time according to your lifestyle.

How It Works: For hypnotics to quit smoking, you need to quit smoking. Hypnosis can work in two ways. The first is to help you find the correct and valid alternative measures, and then guide your subconscious mind to form the habit instead of smoking. This may be similar to chewing a piece of gum or taking a walk. The second method is to train your mind to associate tobacco with bad feelings, such as bad taste in your mouth or foul smell in smoke.

Lose Weight

As with smoking cessation, there are not many studies that can confirm hypnosis' effectiveness for weight loss, although some studies have found that hypnosis can reduce moderate weight by about 6 pounds in 18 months. Hypnotherapy is usually most useful when combined with diet and exercise habits.

How It Works: After being hypnotized, your attention will be highly concentrated. This makes you more likely to listen to and respond to suggestions about behavior changes, such as eating a healthy diet or doing more exercise, which can help you lose weight.

What Is Hypnotherapy?

Hypnotherapy, also known as guided hypnosis, is a psychotherapy that uses relaxation and concentration to achieve an enhanced state of consciousness or mindfulness. In other words, it plunges the individual into a "psychedelic" or changed state of consciousness. This therapy is considered to be an alternative therapy that can use your thoughts to help reduce or alleviate various problems, such as psychological distress, phobias, and unhealthy, destructive, or dangerous habits (i.e., smoking and drinking). Hypnotherapy aims to make positive changes when a person is in a coma or asleep (sleeping) state.

Is Hypnosis Used in Psychotherapy?

Yes, sometimes more accurately, hypnosis is a form of hypnotherapy, which is a form of psychotherapy. As a result, hypnosis is sometimes used to relax the patient or client during the consultation process. In this case, a well-trained psychologist will put the individual in a state of hypnosis or a "dazed" state so that he/she can openly and safely explore the pain and trauma that tend to be "hidden" from consciousness depressing memory. This "change" in mindfulness can help individual patients or clients to view real-life situations, feelings, and events from a "different perspective," namely relationship problems, tension or stage fright, work conflicts, and even chronic pain. When "in a case of hypnosis," a person is more "open" to a hypnotist or psychologists' advice and guidance. As a result, he/she can make positive changes in his/her life.

What Is the Effect of Hypnotherapy?

Hypnotherapy can treat various conditions, problems, and bad/unhealthy behaviors, such as:

- Phobia
- Addiction
- Relationship/family/work conflict
- Sleep disorders
- Anxiety
- Depression
- Post-traumatic stress disorder (ptsd)
- The grief and loss of loved ones
- Quit smoking
- Lose weight

Note: Those with psychotic symptoms (such as delusions or hallucinations) should contact a qualified hypnotherapist or psychologist to determine whether the therapy is correct.

Who Hypnotizes Individuals?

Trained hypnotherapists and psychologists can hypnotize individuals.

What Happens During Hypnosis?

During the hypnosis process, a well-trained hypnotherapist or psychologist uses guided relaxation techniques to stimulate an individual's feelings of extreme relaxation, focus, and concentration to help him/her increase awareness.

What Are the Standard Methods of Hypnotherapy?

The two main methods of hypnotism are suggestive therapy and analysis.

What Is the Recommended Treatment?

Suggested therapy relies on the individual's ability to respond to a hypnotherapist or psychologist's advice and guidance while in a hypnotic state or changing state. This method is usually used to control or prevent harmful or unhealthy behaviors, such as smoking, gambling, nail-biting, and overeating. Research shows that it may also be beneficial for those with chronic pain. Furthermore, research shows that suggestive therapy may encourage positive, healthy behaviors such as self-motivation and self-confidence. This method can help the client or patient "discover" the psychological root cause of the problem or symptom, for example, a person's social anxiety, depression, and past trauma. It must be understood that feelings or memories related to injuries are often "hidden" in a person's subconscious so that the individual will not (on a conscious level) remember the trauma he/she experienced.

What Is the Analysis of Hypnotherapy?

On the other hand, it turns out that analysis is very useful for "Dipping" into the subconscious to obtain repressive memories of past traumas, all of which can lead to psychological distress, mental health conditions, and problematic behaviors. This method is also called "regression therapy," which is more exploratory. The primary purpose of the analysis is to determine the root causes, problems, disorders and symptoms of personal distress. In the analysis process, the psychologist first puts the individual in a relaxed state to hypnotize the individual. He/she then helps the individual explore past events in his/her life. The goal is to explore the individual's subconscious memory of the games so that he/she can get past them.

Disclaimer: This method is not intended to cure or directly "change" personal behavior. Instead, the goal is to identify the leading cause of personal distress and treat it through psychotherapy.

Should I Hire A Hypnotherapist?

It depends on what your doubt is and what you want to solve. The fact is that research has just begun to claim that hypnotherapy can solve psychological problems. For those who want to break the "bad habits," face the trauma of the past, remember that their minds deliberately "forget," relieve chronic emotional and physical pain, and relieve life stress, it has only recently become a mainstream treatment. Therefore, research shows that this alternative psychotherapy may be extremely beneficial for a wide range of psychological, physical, and behavioral problems. However, it must be noted that although hypnotherapy is considered a complementary or alternative therapy, it is still a highly regulated legal, psychological therapy that can sometimes be used to help people cope with painful events. It can also be used to relieve physical, mental, emotional, behavioral (such as smoking, addiction, weight loss or nail biting) and psychological symptoms (such as stress, anxiety, hyperactivity, post-traumatic stress disorder, phobias, and depression), so, individuals (regardless of age) can lead a happy and productive life. In some people, it has also been shown to be effective in treating addiction. Ultimately, however, hypnotherapy aims to help individuals deepen their understanding of themselves.

What Should I See for In A Hypnotherapist?

The methods and hourly rates (costs) used by hypnotherapists to hypnotherapists and psychologists to psychologists vary. This form of psychotherapy is a trust-based activity that requires a lot of time, training, skills and energy. Moreover, this requires a lot of personal input. Therefore, it is vital to interview several hypnotherapists and psychologists to see which type of person matches your temperament and personality. Moreover, it will make you feel at ease in front of him/her. Trust is an essential part of hypnotherapy, so you must trust the people who bring you to the "bottom." Ask for a reference. Don't forget to ask about the education and experience of the hypnotherapist or psychologist (how long has he/she been hypnotized, the percentage of successful cases). This is particularly true if you decide to have hypnotherapy with a psychologist. Ensure that the psychologist has a lot of hypnosis training and experience – and has obtained certification and license in the field.

How to Benefit from Hypnotherapy

Hypnosis is a mental state where attention is enhanced. Hypnotherapy is a psychotherapy that can be used to treat mental illness and medical conditions. Hypnotherapy is used to handle pain, IBS, depression, and addictive diseases. During hypnotherapy, a licensed professional can help you relax to a focused mental state, where you can use instructional images or suggestions to help you overcome some conditions. By entering a relaxed state, accepting advice, and getting help from a professional hypnotherapist, you can make the most of hypnotherapy.

Seek Professional Help

Talk to Your Doctor. You may need to discuss hypnotherapy with your doctor before seeking treatment. Not all health experts will be aware of or support hypnotherapy as an alternative therapy. If your doctor is involved in the clinical results of hypnosis, they may help you get treatment.

- Hypnotherapy is not suitable for all conditions and patients. Be sure to check your health to see if hypnotherapy can help your situation.

- Your doctor can refer you to well-known hypnotherapy therapists in your area.

- Say to your doctor: "I understand how many medical professionals are using hypnotherapy to treat IBS. What do you think about this?" or "Doctors are using hypnotherapy to treat addictive diseases. I think this may be for me. Very appropriate. What is your opinion on this?"

Find A Therapist Practicing Hypnotism. There is no hypnotic rule. This means that not everyone who is "certified" or provides hypnotherapy can be trusted. The best way to ensure that you get the right treatment from a professional is to find a licensed psychologist, therapist, psychiatrist, social worker, or other mental health professional trained by a well-known organization. Search for people interested in hypnotherapy.

- Experts who use hypnotherapy may not be in your area. You may require to search the Internet or professional therapist associations to find nearby institutions.

- Ensure that the therapist has received medical or psychological training. Ask if they are licensed in your land, and where they obtained their degrees, training, and licenses. Find out if they are part of professional organizations.

- Discuss their experience in hypnotherapy and the time they spent on hypnotherapy. Also, ask for a referral. Since hypnotherapy training is not standardized, the condition of any practitioner may vary significantly.

- Consult your doctor, hospital, or clinic, and refer to a hypnotherapist. Talk to any friends and family members to find out if they know any hypnotherapists in your area. Search online to find a therapist specializing in hypnosis, and read other peoples' reviews about that therapist.

Contact Professional Organizations. If you have trouble finding a hypnotherapist in your area, you may need to contact a licensed agency. Organizations are specializing in hypnotherapy, where you can find information, research, benefits, and practicing professionals.

Go Through Hypnotherapy

Stay Hypnotized. If you have any thoughts or beliefs about the effects of hypnotherapy, you can just seek hypnotherapy. If you consider hypnosis is stupid and won't work, you probably won't get any benefits. Before the meeting starts, don't try to learn all about hypnosis, but it's better to keep an open mind without expectations. To enter a state of hypnosis, you must plunge yourself into a state of deep relaxation.

- Some people are more vulnerable than others. Those who strongly doubt or resist are the least likely.

Enter A State of Relaxation. The therapist will start the meeting by helping you get into a comfortable, calm state, keeping your attention focused and open. They may talk to you in a quiet, soothing voice because they will guide you to relax. They may remind you of a single image that helps to enhance the sense of relaxation.

- Part of getting into a state of overall relaxation is to feel safe in your place. This is why you require to trust your therapist.

- For example, your therapist may claim you to close your eyes while listening to calm music. They will count down from ten, and each number requires you to relax more and more muscles. You will let the pressure release from your body. Then you may be asked to think about a peaceful lake and make your thoughts reflect this calm state.

Use Guide Images. One of the keys to hypnotherapy is to use descriptions in your mind. During the hypnosis process, you may be relaxed and calm, concentrating on handling the account. You will visualize certain situations, usually detailed images of your condition, and then try to change the image in your mind from a negative state to a positive state.

- For example, if you suffer from chronic injury, you may be asked to visualize the pain. You might imagine that your pain is a huge red ball. In a hypnotic state, you will be required to think of your pain as something different, such as something less powerful and threatening. Your mind may reimagine the pain, like a small pool of water or a small blue ball rolling slowly on the floor.

Open Suggestions. Another part of hypnosis is being free to the mind in a state of concentration and relaxation. These suggestions are provided by licensed professionals. Before the anesthesia, you and your therapist will discuss your goals and the advice you want to get under hypnosis.

- You can always control the recommendations made to you. Hypnosis is not a kind of mind control. This is one of the principal reasons to find a qualified and trustworthy hypnotherapist.

- For example, under hypnosis, your therapist may say: "You are not interested in cigarettes. You don't want to pick up cigarettes. You have no urge to smoke."

Let Yourself Fall into The Subconscious Mind. Hypnosis can also allow you to identify potential problems that may prevent you from performing operations or make you shrink. Under anesthesia, you can re-examine past events and experiences to understand yourself and your habits better.

- Hypnosis can help you stop criticizing yourself and open yourself to things that you might usually overlook or learn more about yourself.

- For example, your therapist may suggest you check carefully and find memories uncomfortable under normal conditions. You can think about these memories calmly and observe them safely. When you are out of hypnosis, you and your therapist can discuss thoughts and their effects on you.

- If memory work is an essential aspect of hypnotherapy, please be careful. Many studies have shown that memories recalled under hypnosis are usually false memories.

Hypnotherapy to Treat Specific Diseases

Use Hypnotism to Fall Asleep. Research shows that hypnotherapy can help you get deeper and better sleep. You can listen to tapes of hypnotherapy before going to bed to calm and relax your mind and then fall asleep, for those who are prone to hypnosis. They find that sleep better after hypnotherapy before going to bed.

- Hypnotherapy may be a method for people who have difficulty sleeping. This may be a way for them to fall asleep and get more rest.
- Hypnosis has no side effects, which is different from the medicines you need to sleep.

Try Hypnotherapy For IBS. Hypnotherapy has been used for some patients with IBS. Research conducted has shown that IBS patients have fewer symptoms and continue to improve in the years following hypnotherapy. The patient underwent hypnotherapy for one hour for 12 weeks.

- With hypnotherapy for IBS, you may be asked to visualize the intestines as red, inflamed tangles. Under hypnosis, your therapist may suggest that you reimagine the gut as something positive. You can change the image to a pink, smooth rope, which helps your mind overcome the symptoms.

- Discuss the use of hypnotherapy with your doctor. If your doctor is in doubt, please contact a therapist or hypnotherapist to discuss how hypnotherapy can help your IBS.

Deal with Pain. Hypnotherapy has been used to treat chronic pain associated with fibromyalgia, arthritis, and cancer. Hypnosis can also help migraines. Hypnosis can help you get rid of negative emotions and stress that can sometimes be related to chronic pain. When you learn to get rid of pain, it can also help you feel more powerful.

- Hypnosis helps divert attention from pain to other areas, allowing you to control your thoughts, reducing the importance of grief.

Fight Anxiety and Depression Through Hypnosis. Hypnotherapy is used to relieve the stress associated with medical procedures such as surgery and childbirth, and hypnosis aims to help alleviate the fear and pain in this situation. Psychologists began to use hypnotherapy to treat anxiety, depression, and phobias.

- Hypnotherapy may help improve nerve habits, such as nail-biting. The advice under hypnosis may help you overcome your phobia.
- Although hypnosis can help relieve anxiety, you need to face more and more challenging situations.

Try Hypnosis to Lose Weight. Hypnosis can help lose weight and overeating. In addition to weight management programs, hypnosis can change your attitude towards weight loss, diet, and exercise. It can also help you learn how to control your weight while achieving your goals.

- Hypnosis can also help improve self-esteem and body image.
- Hypnosis can help you accept your body at every stage of weight loss.

Think About the Hypnosis of a Child. Hypnosis may be beneficial for children with certain neurological diseases. For example, hypnosis has been used to solve bedwetting, stuttering, thumb sucking, phobias, sleepwalking, and even confidence problems. Children usually respond well to hypnosis.

- Hypnosis can help children discover misunderstandings and understand their meaning.

- Hypnosis may help solve behavioral problems in children and adolescents.

Consider Hypnotherapy in Other Situations. Hypnosis can also be applied to treat other diseases. These diseases include chronic diseases such as smoking, skin diseases, hemophilia, hot flashes, nausea, and vomiting. If you have any medical condition and want to try other treatments, please consider discussing the possibility of hypnotherapy with your doctor.

- Hypnotherapy is not suitable for all situations. Discuss with your doctor and a trained hypnotherapist.

How Can Hypnotherapy Solve the Symptoms of Panic and Anxiety?

Research shows that hypnotherapy can help relieve stress, fear, and anxiety. It can also help cope with the symptoms of panic disorder. Under hypnosis, patients with panic disorder may be guided to deal with specific symptoms and overcome restrictive behaviors. For example, once the hypnotist helps the client relax, he may ask the person to focus on their panic attack. This person will make people aware of the physical sensations, emotions and cognition of their episodes, such as chest pain, shaking and fear. The hypnotist will use encouraging words such as "I feel safe despite the discomfort" or "Anxiety can be controlled."

Hypnotherapy can also be used to treat panic disorder (a common condition in patients with panic disorder). The panic disorder includes fear of panic attacks under controlled conditions (including crowds or while driving). Hypnotherapy can enable a person to learn how to stay relaxed in the face of these fears. A hypnotist can help people focus on getting rid of their phobia and suggest ways to stay comfortable in a fearful environment. Hypnotherapy can help patients with panic disorder improve their self-esteem, overcome negative thinking, and resolve troublesome symptoms.

Treated with Hypnotherapy

Hypnotism can be performed by a qualified hypnotist or a qualified mental health professional trained in this method. Skilled hypnotists can be found through online resources, such as the American Committee for the Qualification of Clinical Hypnotherapists (NBCCH), the American Society of Clinical Hypnosis (ASCH), and the American Association of Professional Hypnotherapists (AAPH). The entire hypnotherapy experience may vary from person to person. Many people have reservations about hypnotherapy, worrying that they will lose control of their thoughts and behavior. Considering how the frequency of hypnotherapy in the media makes people act crazy and stupid, these concerns are understandable. Despite these negative connotations, hypnotherapy cannot make you go against your will. On the contrary, hypnotherapy helps build self-awareness and overcome bad behaviors. Usually, treatment will involve assisting patients to learn self-hypnosis so that patients can continue to use these techniques on their own.

When considering coping with panic disorder, you must discuss your options with your doctor or mental health provider. If you experience panic disorder symptoms, including frequent worry, panic attacks and nervousness, please contact your doctor. Only qualified mental health professionals can provide you with an accurate diagnosis. Hypnotherapy may not be suitable for everyone. People's ability to use hypnosis may vary. People with certain mental health conditions, such as dissociative diseases, active substance abuse, and specific requirements of psychotic illnesses, may not be suitable for hypnosis. Your doctor can recommend that you include hypnotherapy in your panic disorder treatment plan.

Is Hypnotherapy Effective for Weight Loss?

For people who want to lose weight, hypnosis is more effective than diet and exercise alone. Thoughts can influence thinking and change eating habits, such as overeating. However, it remains to be debated how effective it is. An earlier trusted source of controlled trials examined the weight loss effects of hypnotherapy in patients with obstructive sleep apnea. Looked at two specific forms of hypnotherapy and simple dietary advice to reduce weight and sleep apnea. All 60 participants lost 2-3% of their weight within three months. During the 18-month follow-up, the hypnotherapy group lost an average of 8 pounds. The researchers concluded that although this additional loss is unimportant, hypnotherapy deserves more research to treat obesity. Reliable analysis of weight loss, including hypnotherapy, especially cognitive behavioral therapy (CBT), shows that it can be slightly compared with the placebo group. The researchers concluded that although hypnotherapy may reduce weight, there is not enough research to be convincing. It is essential to note that there is not much research supporting weight loss hypnosis. You will find most hypnotherapy combined with hypnosis, diet, exercise, or counseling.

Hypnotherapy Expectations

During hypnotherapy, your therapist may begin your treatment by explaining how hypnosis works. Then, they will check your personal goals. From there, your therapist may start to speak in a soothing, gentle voice to help you relax and build a sense of security. Once your receptivity improves, your therapist may suggest ways to help you change your diet or exercise habits, or achieve your weight loss goals in other ways. The repetition of certain words or specific phrases may help this stage. Your therapist can also help you change yourself and achieve your goals by sharing vivid mental images. To end the session, your therapist will help you get out of hypnosis and return to the original state. The duration of hypnosis sessions and the total number of sessions you may need will depend on your personal goals. Some people may only need one to three sessions to see the results.

Types of Hypnotherapy

There are different types of hypnotherapy. Suggested treatments are more common in habits such as smoking, nail-biting, and eating disorders. Your therapist can also use hypnotherapy with other therapies (such as nutritional advice or CBT).

The Cost of Hypnotherapy

The cost of hypnotherapy varies depending on where you live and the therapist you choose. Consider discussing price or sliding ratio options in advance. Your insurance company may pay 50% to 80% of the treatment provided by a licensed professional. Likewise, please call to learn more about your coverage. You can find qualified therapists by consulting your attending doctor or by searching the provider database of the American Association of Clinical Hypnosis.

Advantages of Hypnotherapy

The benefit of hypnosis is that it allows people to enter a relaxed state of mind, making them more willing to accept suggestions to change certain habits. For some people, this may mean faster and more significant results, but not everyone. If hypnosis is performed under the guidance of a well-trained therapist, hypnosis is safe for most people. This is not a means of brainwashing or controlling the mind. The therapist cannot control a person to do something embarrassing or against their will.

The Risks of Hypnotherapy

Likewise, hypnosis is safe for most people. Adverse reactions are rare. Potential risks include:

- Headache
- Dizziness
- Drowsiness
- Anxiety
- Distress
- Wrong memory creation

People experiencing hallucinations or delusions should consult a doctor before attempting hypnotherapy. Also, do not hypnotize individuals under the influence of drugs or alcohol.

Other Tips for Weight Loss

Some things you can do at home to help you lose weight:

- During most of the week, please move your body. Try 150 minutes of moderate exercise (e.g., walking, water aerobics, gardening) or 75 minutes of vigorous exercise (e.g., running, swimming laps, hiking on the slopes) every week.

- Keep a food diary. Keep count of how much you eat, when you eat, and whether you eat because of hunger. Doing so can help you identify habits to change, such as boring snacks.

- Eat fruits and vegetables. Get servings of fruits and vegetables every day. You should also add more fiber to your diet-25 to 30 grams per day-to suppress appetite.

- Drink six to ten glasses of water a day. Supplementing water helps prevent overeating.

- Resist the urge not to eat. Eating throughout the day helps maintain a healthy metabolism.

Takeaway

Although hypnotism may have advantages over other weight loss methods, it may not be a quick solution. Nonetheless, research does show that combining it with a nutritious diet, daily exercise, and other treatments may help. For more support, please consider consulting your doctor to recommend it to a dietitian or other professional who may help you develop a personal weight loss plan to achieve your goals.

Benefits of Hypnotherapy

Have you ever imagined that a Swami with his head swaying in front of him said that you were sleepy? Hypnosis has been portrayed as a source of entertainment. However, in a clinical sense, hypnotherapy can be used to treat various diseases. But before considering hypnotherapy, you need to understand how it works and what it can and cannot do. When played by a licensed practitioner, the individual usually benefits the most. Hypnosis allows us to focus on the cause of the problem, both physically and emotionally. In turn, it teaches us self-discipline and better-coping methods. Hypnotherapy, especially quantum therapy, can take you back to your previous life and solve your problems.

Kick Bad Habit

Breaking habits is never easy. Even with all the treatments currently available, it is difficult to quit smoking. However, many people can finally break the pattern through hypnosis. Through one-to-one courses, hypnotherapists can customize classes that suit your lifestyle. For hypnotherapy to work, you need to change your nicotine habits. The process is relatively simple. A hypnotherapist can help you find effective alternatives to the effects of smoking. Under guidance, you will subconsciously train your mind to associate smoking behavior with unpleasant feelings.

Lose Weight

Losing weight is an uphill battle for several people. This requires perseverance and dedication. Although some people have achieved their goals, it is almost impossible for others. Hypnotherapy can help people change their eating habits and attitudes, making it easier to eat on time, even for a few seconds.

Treat IBS

Irritable bowel syndrome (IBS) affects millions of people every year. To their frustration, doctors often cannot find a cause or solution. Through progressive relaxation techniques, you will learn how to conceive soothing images to reduce the most common IBS symptoms, diarrhea, constipation and bloating. Also, IBS can cause secondary symptoms such as fatigue, nausea, and even urinary problems. Hypnosis has also been shown to relieve these symptoms.

Improve Sleeping

Hypnotherapy can also help with sleep difficulties. With well-trained relaxation techniques, people with insomnia and frequent waking will generally improve their sleep hygiene. You have a habit of sleepwalking; hypnosis can teach you to wake up before stepping on the floor. If you want to sleep better, hypnotherapy can help you. Learning self-hypnosis strategies can extend your sleep time and deep restorative sleep time.

Relieve Pressure

First of all, it can help you enter a very relaxed state, thereby alleviating tension. If you are in a state of concentration, it will provide advice to your subconscious mind. Learning how to channel your subconscious mind and reduce stress levels can improve your overall health, even if it does not save your life. Facts have proved that stress can cause many chronic diseases, including weight gain, high blood pressure, and cardiovascular disease.

Reduce Chronic Pain Symptoms

There are many forms of chronic pain. Some people suffer from migraines, while others suffer from joint and muscle pain, such as arthritis or fibromyalgia. Hypnotism again teaches you how to cope with anxiety and ultimately control it. Hypnotherapy can also help people with chronic low back pain, Lyme disease, or dysmenorrhea.

Treat Anxiety and Depression

Relaxation strategies, including hypnosis, can help reduce anxiety symptoms. Hypnotherapy seems to be more effective for people who are concerned about chronic illness rather than generalized anxiety. Hypnotherapy may help reduce phobias. Phobias are classified as fear of an absolute reality, which does not constitute a real threat. In some people, hypnosis can also treat symptoms of depression. Those with debilitating depression do need psychological intervention. But people with depression and mild depression may improve. The purpose is to prepare your mind to think in different ways. It is important to note that chronic depression and other, more serious mental illnesses can affect someone's physical health. A low mood is much more than a low state of mind. Depression affects the chemicals in the brain and causes feelings of worthlessness, despair, and sometimes even suicidal thoughts. Hypnotherapy should be a complementary therapy, not the only treatment that people with mental illness rely on.

Reduce Hot Flashes

Even though we may be joking, menopause is not an easy task. Although hormone replacement therapy can effectively treat hot flashes, some women cannot tolerate this therapy and its adverse effects. Also, some women prefer to avoid synthetic drugs and prefer other treatments. Hypnotherapy teaches women to effectively treat hot flashes, which can reduce frequency and intensity. You need to learn how to focus on yourself while turning off external stimuli. For many people, especially those with limited health, hypnotism may be the preferred treatment option. Hypnotherapy has almost no side effects, so it is safe to try. Through practice and training, almost everyone can use hypnotherapy to achieve a certain degree of success. The sign is to have an open mind and learn how to open an account.

Hypnosis and Hypnotherapy: What Is the Difference?

Hypnosis is generally considered to be used by performers in comedy or entertainment activities and is usually regarded as fun and harmless. However, hypnosis has a broader application in helping practice. Often, there are three leading anesthesia platforms:

1. Hypnosis is used for entertainment.
2. Hypnosis is used by people who have been trained for specific purposes, such as helping people quit smoking, control weight, or solve sleep problems.
3. Anesthesia, which is used by a licensed mental health doctor (hypnotherapist) as one of the tools in the counseling/treatment toolbox.

Hypnotism and hypnotherapy have a full history because trained and skilled hypnotists use popular treatment methods. The contrast between hypnosis and hypnotherapy is that hypnosis is defined as a mental state, while hypnotherapy is the name of a treatment that uses anesthesia. Well-trained hypnotists use hypnosis to help people who have problems with smoking cessation and weight management but are not licensed to perform hypnotherapy. Hypnotherapy is performed by hypnotherapists who are trained, licensed and certified professionals. Only hypnotherapists can use hypnotherapy to deal with mental health problems such as phobias, stage fright, eating disorders and certain medical conditions.

How Does Hypnosis Work?

Hypnosis is defined as a harmless trance state characterized by intense relaxation, high concentration of attention and extreme openness to recommendations that are usually positive and promote positive treatment changes. However, a hypnosis trance itself does not necessarily have a therapeutic effect. For example, when someone drives to a shopping mall, seems to arrive suddenly and is not sure how exactly he/she got there so quickly, he/she experiences a changed hypnotic state. When people start to fall asleep and are in a dreamy and sleepy state, they may also experience this altered state, they realize but are not fully focused, only focus on simple conversations and don't remember to speak at all. When used in treatments, specific suggestions and images can positively change their behavior. In this hypnotic state, you are more inclined to make permanent changes and are more likely to succeed in making the lasting changes you want. Almost all lasting shifts happen in your subconscious mind. Another example of how visualization works in hypnotism is when a hypnotherapist helps a person experiencing claustrophobia in a very open space without worrying when entering an elevator. By imagining entering the elevator with no doubt and certainty, one can usually do this in reality. The subconscious mind cannot distinguish between a real experience and a suggested experience. If you observe it in its state, your body will react to it.

Who Can Be Hypnotized?

The most direct answer is that almost everyone can be hypnotized. Modern research shows that most people can be captivated to some extent, and the real problem is the depth and breadth of their troubles. Being able to be hypnotized is not a sign of a weak mind, a tendency to be deceived or giving up control. The ability to captivate (or "hypnotic ability") is related to intelligence and the ability to have increased awareness and concentration under complete control. For example, if you are required to give a hypnotists' wallet or take off all your clothes under hypnosis, you will not do it unless you want to. Likewise, if you are a hypnotist in the audience of stage performance and are selected to perform, you will quack like a duck only when you want it. Participants are chosen because the hypnotist thinks you want to act stupidly and become one of them. This is in contrast to people who do not indicate that they wish to participate in activities or even play.

What Happens to Hypnotherapy?

Like any therapy, hypnotherapy begins with a conversation about what the client wants to achieve in the process. Once the goal is clear, the therapist will understand your identity and can begin hypnosis. The therapist may use certain techniques, speaking in a calm voice or allowing you to visualize relaxing images. For example, make you enter a more relaxed and more receptive state. Once you are calm and focused, the therapist will make a statement and ask questions designed to guide you in achieving your treatment aims. Many people hesitate to see a hypnotist because they are afraid of embarrassing themselves or being controlled by others. Fortunately, these fears are unfounded, hypnosis does not work like this. During hypnotherapy, you can manage your work, and after waking up from the hypnotic state, you will have a clear understanding of the whole process. You can't do anything you don't want to do, and you will fully understand what is happening throughout the process.

Is Hypnotherapy Effective?

Although some scientists and medical professionals are skeptical of hypnotherapy, more and more reliable scientific studies have proved that this technology can help people. Although we need to analyze this nature further to determine the specific advantages and limitations of hypnotherapy fully, the existing evidence is promising. As a result, the medical community has gradually begun to accept this exciting technology as a safe and effective way to improve peoples' lives.

What Are the Best Concerns for Hypnotherapy?

Hypnotherapy can help people with various health problems. These involve anxiety disorders and phobias, depression and sleep problems, trauma, sadness and daily stress. On the other hand, hypnotherapy can also be used to help people change bad behaviors, such as smoking, nail-biting, overeating, and drug use. Ultimately, hypnotherapy is used as an adjunct to medical procedures. It can help anesthesia during surgery or dental surgery, such as more general pain control. Hypnotherapy can also be used to treat irritable bowel syndrome, high blood pressure, allergies, and eczema.

How Do Hypnotherapy Specialists Train?

Hypnotherapists are usually doctors, psychologists, social workers, or family therapists who have received additional training in hypnotherapy through reputable institutions or experienced practitioners. The hypnotherapist should have completed a certification course that includes a lot of working hours.

Concerns/Limitations of Hypnotherapy

Generally, hypnotherapy is considered a very safe technique. However, sometimes it can cause headache or dizziness and nausea. Also, people who have had symptoms of psychosis should not be hypnotized. These usually occur in diseases such as schizophrenia, transient psychosis, and bipolar disorder. It is also necessary to remember that hypnosis should complement other forms of medical or psychiatric treatment, not be used to replace them. Finally, hypnotism has been used to expose repressed experiences in early life that may produce "false" memories and has been criticized. This is because a person in a hypnotic state is in a suggestible state, and sometimes may believe that certain events have occurred, even if not necessary. For undiscovered memories, it is essential to admit that these memories may have symbolic or metaphorical value, rather than real events.

An Important Practitioner of Hypnotism

Sigmund Freud is known as the father of psychoanalysis; he is keen to use hypnotism to restore suppressed memories. Freud adopted this technique because his mentor, Josef Breuer, believed that hypnotism could be used for treatment. However, Freud stopped using hypnosis later, instead of focusing on the use of free association. He believes that the movement of planets will affect human behavior, and there is an exchange of energy between animate and inanimate objects. He also proposed that placing hands within a person's field of vision can cause this energy change. To this day, hypnotists still use this technique, called hypnotism. James Braid-Brad is a Scottish doctor who discovered that fixing his eyes on an object puts him in a therapeutic calm, and relaxed state. Braid, a skeptic of hypnosis, coined the term hypnotism, which is now widely known. He is known for making hypnotism more credible in the medical world.

Methods of Hypnotherapy to Treat Depression

Depression is usually a response to painful or traumatic events. People and situations related to traumatic events in our lives are called trauma triggers. One example is that someone reported: "I never felt frustrated before my father (mother, child, spouse, best friend)." After the death of a liked one, individuals often have to deal with their belongings, including their own house or take responsibility now. Any of these can be a traumatic inducement. If the person who has lost a loved one or family member has no time to feel sad for the lost person and cannot deal with the person's unfinished feelings, depression may occur immediately. Other traumatic triggers include unemployment, divorce, or financial regression, such as bankruptcy or foreclosure.

How Does Clinical Hyperthermia Treat Depression?

It can help you enter the subconscious: first, we descend from the conscious mind (only 10% of the soul) to the psyche. Now, we are dealing with the whole person, which is 100% of the brain, and not just treating symptoms.

It Can Help You Identify "Unfinished Business"

People often own what Dr. Fritz Perl's calls "unfinished business," no matter what is lost, whether it is a liked one, a job, or a house. These unresolved feelings, such as resentment, regret, blame, anger, intuitive GUI, jealousy, and fear, will be stored in the body and released immediately after the triggering event occurs. Otherwise, they will be deeply buried under the numbness of simultaneous suppression caused by antidepressants, addictive behaviors, and untreated trauma and grief. Clinical hypnotherapy is effective for depression because it eliminates the fundamental basis of depression and completes the unfinished business. Otherwise, the company will continue to be recycled as self-destructive thoughts and behaviors.

It Can Help You "Complete" "Unfinished Business" And Release Stored Emotions/Experiences

With the help of hypnotherapy, we can go deep into these traumatic experiences, memories, and stored emotions to release them from the body and mind. After the hypnotherapy process is completed, the client will report that their depression has been relieved. They have stopped their obsessive thoughts or behaviors, and are ready to return to life.

It Can Help You Replace Trauma with A Positive Attitude

In each recovery process of clinical hypnotherapy, we can replace the terrible, repetitive thoughts that often plague people after experiencing trauma. Positive affirmation works now because the essential emotional release has been completed.

It Can Help You Use the Power of Hypnotic Advice to Achieve Long-Term Improvement

Hypnotherapy provides an effective way to gain the ability of an individual to influence the body. Once the self-destructive thoughts and behaviors are resolved, individuals can begin to use hypnotic cues to improve physical function. Hypnotherapy can help correct restlessness, low energy or libido, headaches, or chronic pain patterns. And people can use hypnotherapy to increase motivation for exercise and eating.

What Is Brainwashing?

Brainwashing is a severe form of social impact that can lead to changes in someone's way of thinking without their consent, and often against their will influenced "brainwashers." The agent will actively destroy the target's identity and replace it with another set of behaviors, attitudes and feelings that play a role in the target's current environment. This effect is invasive and requires complete isolation and dependence on the subject, which is why the most common brainwashing occurs in cult organizations or prisons. The agent needs to have full control of the goals, including sleeping patterns, eating, using the bathroom, and meeting other people's basic needs (depending on the agent's wishes). Most psychologists believe that brainwashing can be done under the right conditions. However, some people think this is impossible, or at least not as effective as described by the media. Many specialists believe that even under ideal conditions, the effect of brainwashing is usually short-term. They said that the victim's old identity was not eliminated but hidden. Once the "new identity" is no longer strengthened, the person's old attitudes and beliefs begin to recover. Some psychologists said that the apparent transformation of these prisoners of war was the result of ordinary torture rather than "brainwashing." The fact that few people have been converted raises a reliability question: Is the brainwashing system a system that produces similar results in different cultures and personality types, or does it depend mainly on the influence of a specific target?

How Brainwashing Works

In psychology, the knowledge of brainwashing (often referred to as thought reform) belongs to the field of "social influence." Social influence occurs each minute of every day. It is a collection of ways in which people can change the attitudes, beliefs and behaviors of others. For example, the compliance method aims to change a person's behavior without caring about his views or opinions. This is the "just do" method. On the other hand, the purpose of persuasion is to change your attitude, or "do it because it will make you feel good/happy/healthy/successful." Educational methods (called "propaganda methods" when you don't believe in what's taught) are a kind of gold with social influence. It tries to influence changes in people's beliefs, following "because you do, so do," knowing that is the right thing. "Brainwashing is a critical form of social influence. It combines all these methods to cause a person's way of thinking to change without others' consent and often against his wishes.

Since brainwashing is an intrusive method of influence, it requires the subjects to be completely isolated and dependent, which is why you often hear brainwashing in prison camps or totalitarians. The agent (brainwasher) must adequately control the target (brainwasher) so that the way of sleeping, eating, using the bathroom and the agent's wishes determine other basic human needs. In the brainwashing process, the agent will systematically decompose the target's identity to no more extended function. The agent then follows it with another set of behaviors, attitudes, and beliefs that play a role in the target's current environment. Most psychologists believe that brainwashing can be done under the right conditions. Some people think that brainwashing is impossible, or at least not as dangerous as described in the media. Precise definitions of brainwashing require the threat of personal injury, and under these definitions, most extremists do not practice real brainwashing because they usually do not physically abuse recruits.

Other definitions rely on "non-physical enforcement and control" as an equally effective means of asserting influence. No matter which definition you use, many experts agree that even under ideal brainwashing conditions, the effect of the process is short-term, the process does not eradicate the old identity of the brainwashing victim, but hides it, once a "new identity" is found. "No longer being strengthened, people's old attitudes and beliefs will begin to return. Some psychologists say that the apparent transformation of American prisoners of war during the Korean War was the result of old torture rather than "brainwashing."

Most prisoners of war in the Korean War did not convert to communism at all, which raises the question of reliability: Will the brainwashing system produce similar results in different cultures and personality types, or does it mainly depend on the influence of the target audience? In the next part, we will study an expert's description of the brainwashing process and determine what made it a goal.

Brainwashing Techniques

The term "brainwashing" was invented by the journalist Edward Hunter during the Korean War to describe the "re-education" technique used by the Chinese on captured U.S. troops. The term has since been associated with cults, which often use a combination of psychological methods to make their members obey. Psychologist Margaret Singer argues that at any given time, in the United States alone, about 2.5 million people are members of cults that use brainwashing techniques. But, the idea of brainwashing has always been controversial. Hunter has something to do with the intelligence community. Some people suggested that the CIA promote the term as an easy way to explain the rapid development of communism. Psychologists Robert Lifton or Edgar Schein concluded that most American prisoners of war who made anti-American statements did so to avoid corporal punishment. The brainwashing of prisoners of war was not particularly successful. Therefore, we must be aware that there are some debates about the composition and effects of education.

Singing

The act of chanting is an essential feature of many religions (especially Buddhism and Hinduism), and almost every church has hymns. When each member of the congregation sings or sings the same word, their voices become one, with a strong sense of unity and group identity. Coupled with known singing effects (such as lowering heart rate and relaxing mood), they may actively promote group worship. However, in cult organizations, repeated low tones are intended to numb people, eliminate logical thinking and induce state. This kind of country is characterized by increased suggestiveness. When maintaining a constant state, cults are often punished to ensure the continued implementation of hyper integrationist behavior. Psychologists Linda Dubrow-Marshall and Steve Eichel studied "how repeated hypnosis and prolonged hypnosis can weaken the ability of the converter to make decisions and evaluate new information," adding: "Most cult organizations use continuous lectures. The way of singing and chanting can help to change consciousness." In this way, hypnosis by chanting is a tool used by cult leaders to erode critical thinking skills rather than for meditation purposes.

Isolation

In 1977, approximately 1,000 members of Jim Jones and his People's Temple religious group moved to an isolated commune in Guyana. About 400 kilometers (250 miles) of jungle separated them from the U.S. Embassy in Georgetown, Guyana. As Edward Cromarty pointed out, this isolation helps believers to "no longer pay attention to the values of the outside world," while Jones is free to instill his terrorist regime. Those who question Jones will be put into a drug-induced coma, or even wrapped around their necks by a python. The rebellious child was put down in the well at night. Therefore, the geographical isolation of cults parallels spiritual isolation. The members of the People's Temple are far from being influenced by their relatives and friends in the United States. If they disobey, they will be cruelly punished. The members of the People's Temple have no choice but to listen to Jones' toxic ideology silently. Things feel uncomfortable inside. In terms of total control of its members and forced isolation, the People's Temple's agricultural plan is compared with untouchable countries like North Korea or Albania before 1991.

Dependence and Fear

In 1974, the Communist Liberation Army kidnapped the heiress Patty Hearst, a classic example of relying on dependence and fear for brainwashing. Hearst quickly changed from a young socialite to a bank robber and became a member of a terrorist organization. After Hearst was arrested, she was locked in a cabinet, subjected to physical and sexual abuse and was repeatedly told that she might be killed. SLA completely controls her life. This dependence on the kidnappers leads to the well-known effects of Capture Key or Stockholm syndrome. A few months later, she became an ideological devotee of the organization and even participated in a bank robbery in San Francisco. After the police captured Hearst, the prosecutor refused to admit her brainwashing behavior and argued that she fully complied with the terrorist regulations. Therefore, she was sentenced to seven years in prison. However, President Carter reduced his sentence two years later because of the "degrading experience" the prisoner suffered. Although Hearst may be more impressive than most, her story proves how painful experiences can change our identities and beliefs.

Activity Teaching Method

How can teachers encourage students to behave and obey? The answer is usually to incorporate some physical activities into their teaching. Children will be addicted by jumping or running around on the spot, and the result is exhausted, so they are less likely to quarrel or cause trouble. After realizing this phenomenon, some cult organizations tried to occupy members through a series of tiring activities as a means of control. For example, some suspicious factions, such as Dahn Yoga, are just physical exercise systems on the surface. In Russia, mass sports activities such as aerobics in gymnasiums are recognizable characteristics of the Soviet regime, and historians associate them with repressive state institutions. What separates activity pedagogy from purely physical activity is that a regime or cult organization will use the emotional upswing and group identity experienced after physical activity to introduce ideological beliefs. Otherwise, it may be suspected. Exercising exhaustion is another way to wear down people's defenses to encourage them to accept ambiguities.

Lack of Sleep and Fatigue

The combined effects of feeling overload, disorientation and lack of sleep can impair our ability to make the right decisions. Multi-level marketing company Amway was accused of depriving its distributors of sleep during a weekend event that featured non-stop lectures until the early hours of the morning, during which the band played loud music and flashing lights. A cult method sometimes used in conjunction with rest deprivation involves instructing members to follow a special diet containing small amounts of protein and other essential nutrients. As a result, members of the cult always feel tired, making them unable to resist the cult's ideological instructions. And at the 20th anniversary of the Aim Shinrikyo sarin nervure gas attack, the Japan Times interviewed a former member of the cult. He described "eat one meal a day and sleep for a few hours a night" while trying to make the leader of the cult Elected to Parliament.

Self-Criticism and Blame

When the Korean War, American soldiers captured by China suffered "criticism and self-criticism." They had to condemn their fellow prisoners, discuss their faults and express their insecurities towards capitalism and the United States. At first, the prisoners of war thought these meetings were naive. However, with time, the ongoing criticism began to cause them to express genuine doubts about the effectiveness of patriotism and war. Psychologist Robert Cialdini (Robert Cialdini) will explain that prisoners' growing anxiety is the result of the "rule of promise." The "rule of promise" says that because we don't want to be weird or dishonest, we try to make our ideas, and the public statement remains consistent. Despite some limited success, the "brainwashing" methods were not particularly useful in general. Although at the end of the war, only 23 prisoners of war refused to repatriate, and most of the Chinese gave up repatriation a year before the end of the war. They continue to use similar practices at home.

Love Bombing

Cultists hope to enhance the impression that the world outside the group is threatening and making severe mistakes. To make themselves appear hospitable, they often use "love bombs" to make themselves appear cordial. The love bomb involves swaying a lot of new people or potential recruits and showing attention and affection. The term may have originated from the

Son of God or the Unified Church, but it can now be applied to multiple organizations. We are strongly inclined to socialize with the kindness and generosity of others. This is a common phenomenon in social psychology. Therefore, false love, encouragement and friendship shown by the members of the famous cult towards fellow initiates are aimed at enhancing obligations, debts and guilt. A feature of cults because companionship and confirmation are precisely what many new factions are looking for and, therefore, useful. Psychologist Edgar Schein believes that people are introduced into cults through "thawing and refreezing." During the thawing phase, potential members of the new cult began to reject his old worldview and were open to cult thinking. During the refreeze period, the faction consolidated this new view. Schein pointed out that the love bomb is a critical element of the re-freeze recruits that accept that cult philosophy will be embraced and praised, but if they ask too many doubts, they will avoid it.

Mysterious Manipulation

Psychiatrist Robert Jay Lifton believes that many cults rely on "mysterious manipulation" to control their followers' full control. Mystic manipulation refers to the control of the environment or information by cult leaders to convey the impression that they possess supernatural intelligence, charisma, or magical powers. If a self-proclaimed religious leader promotes himself as a reliable messenger of God, his views must always be accurate and correct and support this with amazing skills and extraordinary heads. David Koresh's early challenge to George Rodden, one of the Davidson branch leaders, dramatically exhumed a corpse in the theater. He pledged to be reborn to prove his witchcraft power. He challenged his competitors and asked to do so, but Koresh only reported his grave robbery. The police requested Koresh to provide evidence. When Koresh's faction tried to enter the compound where Rodden kept the body, a gun battle broke out. Koresh himself was called Vernon Howell at the time but was later renamed to imply the descendants of King David in the Bible. He named Koresh after the surname of Cyrus the Great, the King of Persia, who rescued the Jews from Babylonian imprisonment. Kolas created a messianic character and encouraged his followers to attribute the unusual experience to divine intervention after careful planning.

Brutal Abuse

Many cult organizations hire lawyers to sue anyone who criticizes them publicly, no matter how trivial the criticism is. Of course, the factions can usually bear the responsibility of losing the lawsuit, and former cult members are generally unable to pay their debts after giving their lives to the organization. Therefore, many former missionaries were unable to conduct effective legal counterattacks. Due to the constant threats of legal proceedings, mainstream journalists dare not condemn cults or quote cult materials. In 2003, researcher Rick Ross extracted from NXIVM's manual, NXIVM, a self-improvement organization, was accused of engaging in cult activities. Rose put these passages on the Internet but was hit by lawsuits and investigators who ran around in his trash can. Several NXIVM employees who left the organization are facing severe lawsuits. The judge dismissed one such case and pointed out that the relevant employees were only trying to go and were only "labeled as 'inhibited'."

This meant that NXIVM applied to former partners who went to the company or were regarded as enemies by NXIVM and accepted the two. The protracted litigation of a large law firm and a group of lawyers. "Scientism is also known for using frivolous lawsuits to stop the opposition." L. Ron Hubbard wrote in 1967: "We cannot find scientism critics without a criminal history." The trial should silence these naturally guilty critics. "The purpose of [lawsuit] is to harass and dissuade, not to win." HBO is fully aware of the consequences of troubled scientists, so it hired 160 lawyers to defend its 2015 documentary "Going Clear." Instead of launching a counterattack, the church began a "barbaric" campaign against the characters appearing in the film and director Alex Gibney.

Contemplative Cliché

Another fundamental concept put forward by Robert Jay Lifton is that totalitarian regimes usually rely on "the clichés of the end of thought" to impose obedience to their subjects. Through these clichés, "the most profound and complex issues of human impact are compressed into short, reductive, and certain phrases." Lifton's classic example is the "all-encompassing jargon of communist regimes such as China and the Soviet Union," the language there became "abstract, highly confidential and ruthlessly judged" and eventually became "a language without thought." The Soviets' love for this jargon inspired George Orwell's idea in 1984 that the oppressive government designed a language called "Newspeak" to suppress thinking beyond the terminology defined by the state. New NGOs like the Church of Scientology may have developed a set of phrases that are roughly the same as Soviet jargon.

The most famous example of "the cliché of the end of thought" may come from the trial of Nazi official Adolf Eichmann. The author Hannah Arendt pointed out in her famous work on Eichmann and "evil banality" that S.S. leaders often speak idioms and clichés. Eichmann reiterated time and time again that he wanted to "live in harmony with his former enemies." Despite this, Arendt concluded that the sentence was meaningless because he did not understand the seriousness of his crimes, he could only conceive of these crimes in the language of National Socialism. Arendt concluded that during the war, "the German society of 80 million people has been shielded from reality and facts by the same means, the same self-deception, lies and foolish behavior."

How to Brainwash Someone

If you want to understand how to brainwash someone, take a look at any cult, and you will recognize the process they use to recruit new friends, change their attitudes and beliefs and involve them. Manipulators use the same process in intimate relationships. This is not a manual for people who want to initiate a cult or manipulate others. If this is your intention, and you are not a psychopath or a narcissist (do it anyway!), you may not be able to perform these actions. Often, there is a deliberate lack of empathy and mental illness to deliberately and systematically control/destroy another person. Destruction is the object of brainwashing. This is not just about changing their thinking but also about improving their view of the world, their thinking strategies, emotions, decisions and behaviors. As a result, you change a person's personality or identity to something else. Once completed, these changes will continue for several years, unless the victim intentionally eliminates these changes.

How to Brainwash Someone-Big Picture

- Choose your goal.
- Give them what they want.

- Make them feel special, wanted, loved.
- Then give attention, condition their behavior, and think about what you want.
- Switch what they wish to to something bigger. (Then switch it to what you want)
- Criticizing them will start to unfreeze their personalities.
- Separate them from the bottom of the world and the past, so you become their primary source of information.
- Use fear and guilt to make them think and make decisions in different ways.
- Keep them busy physically and mentally, so they don't have time to think and disrupt normal functions such as sleep and eating.
- Let them rely on you and install a phobia.
- Use bonuses and punishments to freeze new ideas, beliefs, and behaviors.
- Wash, rinse, repeat.

Although I have listed these in this order, sometimes there may be considerable overlap between them. It may be necessary to jump from one step to another, or go back and repeat several levels, and there may be multiple items happening at the same time and so on. These stages occur in cults, work environment, social status and intimacy, although they seem to be different in each situation. Let's look at each in more detail.

How to Brainwash Someone-Provide

Worship has a facade that can be used to attract members. It can be private development, religion, health, politics, sports, or any other thing. People do not participate in cults, and they will participate in sales training courses, or improve their relationships or lose weight. Each group has something that they provide for people. They find that this is unique to that group. You can't get similar things anywhere else, and you have the hope of realizing your dreams. Although their target group seemed to be specific, members were quickly assumed that the group would work for almost anyone. They act accordingly, trying to invite everyone. In an intimate relationship, "what is offered" is variable. The manipulator can quickly evaluate goals and determine their own needs, desires, fears, weaknesses and even strengths. Then, the manipulator will provide the victim with what the victim wants. This can be anything from work to the company, to help solve problems, to a place of accommodation, to advice, to a crying shoulder, to the relationship between marriage and the hope of children. In either case, the victim was deceived. Manipulators hide all kinds of information, lie bluntly, and sprinkle with sugar to make them more delicious.

How to Brainwash Someone-Bombing

Once the person attends the group meeting, they will be killed. This means that group members make them feel very welcome, unique, caring, smart, talented and even loved. This has a powerful impact on new friends and immediately makes them feel like they have met instant friends and become part of the team. It makes it easy for the original victim to share information about themselves and take the next step, and it is also difficult not to take further steps! Even if "more" is not what you want, it is challenging to refuse more services from such a lovely person. The same process applies to intimate relationships. Make the victim feel that he has met the perfect partner. The newcomer seems to tick all the boxes. The victim feels accepted, understood and loved. The victim opened and revealed his details to the robot. The purpose of this love bomb is to make the victim committed to further participation in the relationship in a cult, one-on-one situation, or work environment.

How to Brainwash Someone-Not Paying Attention

In a cult organization, although people usually focus on groups (health, sales, nutrition, etc.), group rules are introduced. Sometimes it is done in public, often in secret. The fresh member notices that doing certain things will alienate another member in a certain way while doing other things brings more pleasant and careful attention. Novices quickly learned that to feel good and maintain a friendly demeanor for the leader and team and they must think and act in a certain way. In this way, the beliefs and behaviors of members are shaped by the group.

In an intimate relationship, all unconditional love suddenly becomes conditional at the beginning of the relationship. The victim learned that doing certain things would make the "ideal partner" unhappy and quickly adjusted to solve it again. The victim realized that what was acceptable at the beginning was no longer the case. The terms and circumstances of the relationship are adjusted by the manipulator, so if the victim wants to be treated well, they must change the relationship with the manipulator. No one likes to be treated silently, mainly when the link (so far) is based on love, happiness, and mutual understanding. The motivation to avoid withdrawing such careful attention is powerful.

How to Brainwash Someone-Change Focus

Soon after becoming a group member, new members are guided through a series of procedures to transform what initially attracted them to join the group into a desire for more substantial things. The general idea of selling to them is: "Please note how satisfied you are with what we are doing here. Imagine if more people knew about it. Will the world get better? Wouldn't it? In this way, people who lose weight start to take the product, and then they get an idea that if they sell the product themselves, they can benefit from the product while making money. People who participate in seminars to improve their communication skills are better at starting to strengthen their identity. If they do, their communication skills will naturally improve. They are believed to turn to create an "ideal self" for their overall benefit."

Another person who wanted to establish a personal relationship with God was told that their relationship included going out to spread. They asked: "Now, you don't want to make God sad, do you?" They are further used to recruit members. In an intimate relationship, the manipulator's common strategy is to make everything related to the relationship. "I am doing this for the advantage of the link. What are you doing for us? Do you want this relationship to continue?" Later, the leader, whether it is a cult or an intimate relationship, turned his attention. The cult leader pointed out that the higher goal that the victim can achieve can only be achieved through him (or her). Members began to believe that unless they have any relationship with the leader, there is no value. To this end, leaders tell stories to increase their importance. They claim to have exclusive rights and secret knowledge and appreciate any good things within 50 yards of them.

How to Brainwash Someone-Personal Criticism

Cults and manipulators in intimate relationships criticize the victims. But this is not just about anything old. They can, of course, use any old things to criticize, but the purpose of criticism is to target their identity and self-awareness. Robots do not criticize behavior, opinions, or beliefs, but directly criticize human behavior or ideas. Instead of saying, "this is a stupid thing," it is better to say, "you are stupid (because of doing this or thinking that)." This is very important because, as these insults are repeated, they profoundly impact the victims. They destroy self-esteem and begin to destroy a person's personality. The victim feels embarrassed and ashamed of who he is and strives to change himself to please the manipulator.

How to Brainwash Someone-Isolation

The robot will do a lot of things to isolate the victim from family and friends and any other support networks. The reason they do this is that they want to be the only source of information for victims. Caring family members will determine the victim that they are the target of a cult or abuse, and the manipulator does not want the victim to know this. The excellent way to prevent this from happening is to keep the victim out of contact with others, or not to understand or accept what friends and family tell them. The robot will say various things to the victims and take action to separate them from outsiders, including telling members that if they don't support them, their family will not love them. Of course, a family will not support a loved one who is worshipped. Nonetheless, usually, when the family realizes what has happened, they are inoculated in any criticism of the group or the leader by the family. In this way, the victim was programmed to not pay attention to anything the family said or actively defend the group. If friends do not join the group, they will be told that they will be stopped by such non-believers and cut off. Members can even change their name, rewrite history, not allow to talk about specific topics or engage in certain activities, must use particular languages, dress in a certain way, adopt appropriate hairstyles or change specific techniques to isolate themselves and adapt to the team's lifestyle. The victims are separated from the outside world, but they are encouraged to spend time with other group members to strengthen their ideas. Members support each other in observing the rules and each other reinforces group beliefs. This helps build the cult's "us to them" mentality.

How to Brainwash Someone-Emotional Control

Cult members are prohibited from being angry or frustrated with the group leader. Any anger will be transferred to the outsider. Fear and inwardness are the two primary emotions used to control people under emotional control. Fear of outsiders, fear of rejection by the team or leader, fear of losing what has been learned, the anxiety of independent thinking and fear of leaving are some of the more common things that make people obey. Internal is another major factor in this situation. Victims often do not know how much crime they have experienced in the environment, but the manipulator repeatedly uses this control mechanism. Leaders must be prepared for everything to go well, and leaders must be ready for all errors. Members are often forced to take personal responsibility for all kinds of things. They fall into an endless loop, trying to improve themselves and prevent bad things from happening to "play their potential." This sense of personal responsibility also destroys people's personalities. Due to the psychological pressure exerted on them, more than one person has become nervous or committed suicide. Fear and inwardness are beautiful combinations that force people to think and make decisions. People will make decisions to avoid anxiety and internalization. In this way, the leader does not always have to tell people what to do. He just has fear and feelings about A so that members can choose B. B, of course, is what the leader wants first, and doing so is the benefit of the leader, that is, the leader thinks the members are doing their own decision.

How to Brainwash Someone

The leader will keep the victim busy, weak and active. In cults, there are repeated exercises, tools to be mastered and techniques to be practiced. There are books, DVDs, audios, etc., which contain a lot of information that needs to be digested. If you have completed all these operations, you will be told that it is worth doing all the services again. Then, you need to check, recheck, rewrite, update, etc. to list your needs, expectations, values and goals. Most importantly, members should tell others, spread information and teach the world. Cults never have a dull moment. It is always necessary to perform analysis to discover deeper meanings, learn valuable lessons and deeply realize this. This is all mental gymnastics. This has no real value for cult members, but its function is to keep them in the cult mentality. In an intimate relationship, the manipulator will keep the victim busy, doing housework, parenting, paperwork, traveling to the bank and the post office. Following the victim's mind actively, the traditional way of manipulators is to tell a fair person that they are low, or a friendly person that they don't care about others, or an honest person that they are a liar.

This usually causes the victim's head to rotate, figuring out the meaning of the manipulator. "Why does she say that? Did she notice something I didn't notice? Do other people think that I am the opposite of me? What am I missing here?" Suppose a cult can keep its members busy, so much the better! A tired person cannot resist the spirit. Moreover, if factions can make people eat a low-protein diet, they will do the same. Now add chanting, dancing, singing, hypnosis and meditation, your people will no longer thoroughly think about it, but they will be quickly advised and manipulated. Cults encourage people to become paranoid about their thoughts and believe that their problems are themselves. The worship will urge members to stop thinking and judging. Members will soon accept the leader's flawlessness and have answers to all the questions in life. They will believe in pseudo-scientific research disguised as evidence and will take all kinds of opinions without any evidence or even questioning. At this stage, they have entered the field of blind obedience.

How to Brainwash Someone-Dependence

Leaders will make their victims depend on them. Criticizing victims for independent thinking and making their own decisions, criticizing their choices, alternately criticizing and praising, attacking people's identity and creating a phobia of leaving are some of the techniques used by cult leaders and manipulators in intimate relationships to build a childlike dependence among the victims. Cult members and other victims often use themselves as co-dependents to explain their reliance on the manipulator. This is an ideological error because it reverses causality. The victims think they have a dependent personality, which is why they finally chose this controller. The truth is that because they are with the manipulator, they become helpless. This is part of the cult character imposed on them.

How to Brainwash Someone-Refreeze

I have described some of the brainwashing techniques used to defrost the victim's personality and how to use various methods to make people think in different ways, make decisions, and take different actions. Once these things are in place, once members of the cult (or partners in intimate relationships) have mastered this new worldview and act and think according to the leader's wishes, a simple method is usually used to freeze this new system of rewards and punishments. The victims acted following the doctrine, and they were rewarded; they violated the "rules" and were punished. In this way, this new personality is frozen and stabilized over time. It becomes the new default value for the victim. This cult personality or pseudo-personality is to obey and be loyal to the leader. If someone criticizes the leader, the procedure is designed to defend the leader. Plan to trust the leader and follow his or her instructions. It is also very dependent on the leader.

The leader becomes the life purpose of the false personality, and the wrong person organizes itself around the leader. The idea of pseudo-personality is very distorted, and it is impossible to identify the leader's control over it. It also does not see contradictions in the team or relationship, such as leaders doing things that members are not allowed to do. Pseudo-personality beliefs are powerful and usually more reliable than ordinary opinions. Under normal circumstances, humans like to keep their thoughts intact, and often ignore or even deny information that contradicts these beliefs. The intensity of the false personality beliefs means that this ignorance or denial of information has been brought into full play among cult members and other psychological abuse victims. This is difficult to convince them that they are in a state of abuse.

How to Brainwash Someone-Wash, Rinse, Repeat

This process keeps happening in cults. Members are always manipulated and abused by leaders to maintain their hypocrisy. At the same time, new members have to join the old members and pass the former members (because the false characters are programmed to recruit and instill new members). Cults like to have members frequently participate in cult activities. In addition to getting money from them, this also provides the leadership with an opportunity to "fill in" the pseudo-personality. Some groups insist that members participate in an activity every six to twelve months to keep their learning and group development in sync. Of course, what happened was that their pseudo-character was strengthened.

As a "punishment" for wrongdoing, other groups ask people to go back to the beginning of the indoctrination process and re-examine things. This has at least two purposes. The first is to punish, and the second is to teach. One essential point to remember is that the techniques, tools and processes of the cult are useful for the products they provide, whether it is making money, becoming healthy, personal development, religion, or other. However, these things have been distorted so that they all brainwash members, destroy their real personalities, and replace them with cult personalities that only think and work for the leader's benefit. At the same time, members believe that the leader is helping them! Canceling this process is a difficult task, and it is best done with the help of professionals.

Ways to Protect Yourself from Emotional Manipulation

All emotions, good or bad, have a purpose in our journey, but beware of those who want to use powerful emotions to manipulate you. If you consider yourself to be a sympathizer, this applies mainly to you, because this group of people is most likely to absorb harmful energy from others. Next time you feel that your emotions are being manipulated, please refer to the following tips to protect your energy field. Ways to protect yourself from emotional manipulation:

Don't Fall into The Trap

People who are willing to play with others' emotions will use any strategy (such as confusion, blame, and questioning) to hide their skin. If you have to deal with these kinds of people often, such as in the workplace, please ignore them, or say something beautiful rather than surprise them, rather than greet them with a fighting attitude. Emotional manipulators will flourish to cheer you up, so make sure you are not offering them what they want after a few failed attempts; they may start to make you feel lonely.

Begin to Write Down What They Said During the Conversation

Although this may seem excessive, the emotional manipulator has a habit of making you look like a wrong person and twisting your own words to fit any schedule. When you become the victim of their terrible plan, you may begin to believe that sometimes you do something wrong. To ensure that you show them what they said in previous conversations, write down any details that you think they might easily change to justify their actions. They may also try to convince you that they have never said yes, but you can prove that you took notes. Smartly protect themselves from danger; they will quickly become discouraged and unable to use you as an emotional toy.

Avoid Turning as Much as Possible

Of course, avoiding emotional operators and instigators will eliminate your chances of being exploited. For this reason, when you first see them, please try to read their energy. If you can't get a pleasant atmosphere from it, please trust your instincts and conclude agreements to eliminate conflicts. Working in the same position as an emotional manipulator can be tricky, but the goal is to restrict interaction with people as much as possible. This way, you will save a lot of energy and sanity.

The Act of Calling Them

These people may have been around others for a long time and have never encountered them. Please stand up for yourself and let them know that they are making you uncomfortable and being used. Also, if they deny their behavior or try to change their behavior, you can at least see that they are defending themselves and defending the facts. If you are upset with them, maybe they will start to change their music. After all, once they panic everyone away, they will have no one to manipulate.

Avoid Emotional Attachment to Them

Easier said than done and especially if they don't immediately show their true colors. Note that their first sign will completely suppress your emotions, slowly move away from the relationship, and let them know your boundaries. Emotional manipulators are continually looking for the next victim, but if you don't invest much in the relationship, you can break up easily. If you must talk to them, please stay cordial and civil participation, but if you value your emotional well-being, don't let it go further.

Meditate Often

To maintain high vibrations, you need to silence your mind, breathe deeply, and get in touch with higher realms to deal with the problems on earth adequately. This will help you deal with emotional manipulators better because no matter how chaotic you are, you will have inner peace. In particular, love meditation will enable you to cultivate compassion for this person and even open your eyes to see what they have experienced in their lifetime. Face hostile emotions with love and understanding, and after a while, you may witness them transforming into a new person.

Inspire Them

"Being changed" is crucial. In this case, it will inadvertently provide you with protection, because they will not exude such a negative atmosphere after your non-manipulative positive actions motivate them. Cultivate the benefits of meditation, be responsible for your own life, follow your true passion, volunteer service, clean your diet, and exercise. Become the best self with all the knowledge gained about being the best self.

Tell Them, "You Are Right"

Despite how hard this is for the ego, your soul will applaud you and even continue to stand up. Emotional manipulators feed on drama, so reaching a consensus will leave them speechless and quickly put out their fantasies. Just to make you worry and let them win the argument. You know that their actions and accusations are wrong, but they will have to deal with this karma anyway.

Let Go of Toxic Relationships

If you find this behavior in your boyfriend, girlfriend, or spouse, you should abandon this relationship to maintain your happiness. No matter how many unstable actions you make, you cannot force them to change. You should get someone who will nurture and balance your emotions, not someone who wants to use you as entertainment.

Develop A Healthy Mindset

Never let their insults or rage enter your mind; laugh at them, or entertain them without agreeing with them. If you know what kind of person you are and have a strong sense of self-worth, then what they say will not disappoint you.

Let Yourself Communicate Actively Throughout the Day

Emotional manipulators can destroy your formerly disturbing emotions, so make sure you recover from uplifting affirmations and messages during the day. They watched happily at their depression, so when they see that you are not affected by their rude remarks, there is no longer any reason to torture you.

How to Beat a Manipulator

Humans can invade. Ask any conman. Our desire to think that we can control our lives often makes us unable to extricate ourselves, but most of us are highly suggestive and hypnotic. If you feel you are not, you are more vulnerable to hacker attacks than someone who is humbled to see how this situation works. Don't be ashamed of being cheated. Realizing that you have been restrained will naturally bring you embarrassment, but it is never your fault that someone takes you for a ride. Figure out: it is a crime to control someone; being imprisoned is the victim of that crime. This is the view of the law in fraud cases. The robot

DARK NLP AND MANIPULATION

will like that you think it is your fault to allow yourself to be manipulated, but this is just another manipulation, isn't it?

When manipulators show sympathy to us, they will use one of our most shocking, useful, and beautiful human features. Our innate trust is why we can collaborate on a large scale to create and innovate in extraordinary ways, which is not seen anywhere else in the animal kingdom. Because we learn through modeling and are influenced by the group, we live and desire to create harmony, which will make our lives uncomfortable until we align with the tribe. We are the creators of peace; we seek arrangements, and this is how we make the manipulators keep up with their sick schedule. What is the ability of a manipulator to control us to sympathize and connect with us? Due to the popularity of mass media, each of us is in an abusive relationship with wealthy manipulators. Many of us have also established personal relationships with manipulators. Conveniently, from the wealthy class to your cohabiting partner, the strategies for dealing with social manipulators are the same.

Clarify Your Wishes

When you don't understand what you want, you can easily be preyed and let others decide. When you don't know who you are and what you mean, anyone can choose it as their sick schedule. Sit down, keep quiet, and make an inventory of who you are and what you need. Don't worry about adding things you don't have yet. This is the point. List the things that you want not only to survive but to thrive. Apply the rules of survival to each of your wishes. When you are sure that what you want will not harm or interfere with anyone else's dreams, then this list is good. You can stick to it unequivocally, and you should do your best to do it. Scale-up and advocate it loudly.

Where to Watch Resources

How do you understand if you are being manipulated? The manipulator understands that what the rest of us don't know is that the funds in real life, such as sex, money, work, gold, oil, land, water, food, people, air, etc. are all excellent feelings. They will always try to make you exchange real things to get a good impression. If you do not have empathy, then you will see the whole world in a completely different way. Most people work to get what they need without hurting anyone because hurting someone also destroys them. Robots don't encounter this situation, so they get what they need by telling the victim that will hurt someone if they don't hand it over. Narrow down and count who owns everything. In which directions are the scales tilted? Good manipulators will work hard to change the foundation below us, channel real wealth into their coffers, and at the same time make us happy about how fortunate our hard work and all this is, and how much health care will be required when there are people in Syria who need to be blown up for their freedom.

Put everything down, zoom in and out, and see who has mastered everything. Who has all the power you can use in the real world, all the wealth, all the real things, who almost does not exist, but who has the hope of a better tomorrow? The same goes for a marriage. Who has all the wealth, power, honor, retirement savings and who has a story about rational people? Religion has made us manipulate, and this is by design. For thousands of years, we have been instructed to cherish loyalty, piety, diligence, obedience and leave judgment and rewards after death. This creates an ideal environment for the manipulators, where they can see what is valuable in the real world and what is woven from fairy tales. Find out the real situation here and now and see who is in control of your belongings. is it you? When this is not the case, then you have been manipulated from it.

Pay Attention to Their Actions, Not Words

The manipulator has only words. They can't just approach you and say: "give me your life savings," they must weave a complicated story to make you think it's right. A good liar will never ask for anything if they can get rid of it. Ideally, they want you to provide a quote. That is the best kind of scam. The victims first think it is their idea. A great liar will make you beg him to accept what he has always wanted, so he can even thank him for it. By zooming in and seeing what they are doing instead of listening to what they are saying, you can better understand what is happening. For example, if they say they are voting for single-payer healthcare, opposing any effort in any direction, using money from donors who oppose it, and expressing support when intervening in general, these are all true stories.

When the offer is not what you want, but you are so desperate, so distant from them, so invested, and therefore canceled from any other solution, you will be able to choose anything, then the scam is complete considered from their perspective. Ideally, they want to be the owner you don't want. They want to be the people you place hope and energy for, so you won't go to someone who will help them. Nevertheless, they need to restrain you for as long as possible, do as little as possible, and get as much energy from you as possible without raising suspicion. They sang "not now, but soon" inertial songs, progressive songs. This is how they get you into trouble. If you zoom in and observe what they are doing, rather than saying what they are saying, you will know when to apologize to Felicia and seek a real solution.

Don't Try to Manipulate Them Too Much

Once figured out, they will be managed, and the subconscious reaction is to try to return them. Dude didn't even know how beautiful and precious this is. These people have no empathy throughout their lives, and there is no emotional interference that casts a shadow over their decisions. They are like a game of chess and cards, and everyone is playing in their lives. They are masters. They are five steps ahead of you, and you just understand what a novice is. They have been manipulating their belts all their lives, and you are such a rookie. You will lose the game. Do not play. Instead, use your advantages. Ask what you want and stick to it persistently. Keep asking what you want in the most direct way. Remember, the purpose of the manipulator is to take your will away from you. Take it back. Many of us have been manipulated for so long. We don't even know what we want. Keep your inventory simple; keep it at the desired level, then stand firm and make demands. At the same time, keep pointing out the strange things they did to avoid telling you what they said when they yelled slyly from the roof. They used your courtesy and kindness to cover up their small mistakes. Don't let them anymore. If they are creepy, please speak up. Don't be acquiesced for being polite.

At least tell yourself the truth, even if the facts don't match your worldview. As for what the known facts are, what are conjectures or wishful thinking, please be as honest as possible. Verify everything as much as possible to let you know that you are in a stable, factual position. Robots like to make people as confused as possible. Get as many quantifiable and verified facts as possible and build your worldview. When you are sure you want to say it, say it is true, because you know it is true. Be straightforward about what you know. When you are confident, do not let anyone enter any creepy room. Curiosity, objectivity and a relaxed attitude to handle your private research, but once the work is done, keep your feet down and don't let them uprooted. Finally, don't follow the rules, follow the correct standards. Robots like rules because they like to develop strategies for how to bend the rules and how to interact with them. Think of the worst lawyer, and you will fully understand what I mean. If you are a perfect person like yourself and always try to put yourself in the highest interest, then you will know if you do the right thing. Believe in your guts and forge ahead. Even if you violate the rules, you must continue to do the right thing.

Rules for The Reverse Application of The Robot

There is something called "projection" in psychology. Anyone who has done a lot of inner work will tell you that this is a convenient tool for self-inquiry to find out whether you hate others and whether you can find yourself. To avoid being internalized, we tend to project things we don't like to others to hide our shame. Exposing it to light usually results in some healthy forgiveness for ourselves and our perception of others. Great, but the sage didn't tell you that people are always projecting at you. If your advice and kindness are enough not to hurt anyone, you can treat everyone's predictions of you as truth without being aware of it. Unless you have a strong, conscious, and healthy sense of who you are, you will angrily think that you are anything terrible that people project on you, and this will quickly get you into confusion and stop. Once again, take an inventory of who you are, what you want, and gradually expand until you can stand up and defend the truth. Find your will and bring it back.

Robots mainly use projection as a strategy to hide everything they do to you. The robot can chase its tail by merely suggesting what you or others are doing, and you just see them doing it with your own eyes. DNC arrested for election manipulation? Oh, no, Russia manipulated the election by choosing the DNC to manipulate the election. See, what am I doing there? It's silly, but it works. This is the key: simply reverse the pronouns. When facing the manipulator, everything he says to you, he is talking about himself, and everything he says about himself is what he thinks of you. If he tells you that you are a liar then you are a liar, and you are trying to take all of him away, he is saying that he is a liar, and boy is he a liar. If you have a reasonable reason to believe that you are being manipulated by someone, reverse the pronouns in your mind and tell you who they are. It ranges from interpersonal relationships to big manipulators hired by the rich.

Raise as much awareness as possible of all the manipulation and the thoughts you unintentionally form. Make yourself as conscious as possible so that all of us can add to the sum of human knowledge about how to transcend these operations. Once we succumb and fill the borders of our sovereignty, we will be able to believe that we stand by our truth. We will also be capable of seeing who we can trust more effectively, and once you know you can trust someone, you can work with them. This new consciousness and divine cooperation will create everything needed to solve the real-world difficulties we face as a kind and take the will of the earth from the hands of human diseases and return it to the will of people. One of the turning points for people who cannot be manipulated and awakened to collaborate to create a new system that will surpass the old system is to take power from the manipulator, who can only use the ancient biblical tools to use fear, inwardness, and shame. This is feasible and only requires you.

How to Recognize Signs of Emotional Manipulation?

Emotional manipulators often use mind games to snatch power in relationships. The ultimate goal is to use this power to control others. Healthy relationships are based on trust, understanding and mutual respect. This is true for both personal and professional relationships. Sometimes people try to use these elements of the relationship to help themselves in some way. The symptoms of emotional manipulation can be subtle. And it is often difficult to identify them, especially when they happen to you. We will review the common forms of psychological manipulation and how to recognize them.

They Maintain "Home-Court Advantage"

Whether you are in your actual home or just your favorite coffee shop, being in your home can make a difference. If other people always insist on meeting in their field, they may try to create a power imbalance. They claim ownership of the space, which puts you at a disadvantage.

E.g.:

- "If you can, come to my office. I'm too busy to trek to you."
- "You know how far it is to drive. Come here tonight."

They Got Too Close Too Fast

In the traditional "know you" stage, emotional manipulators may skip some steps. They "shared" their darkest secrets and loopholes. But what they are doing is trying to make you feel different so that you can reveal your secrets. They can use these sensitivities on you later.

E.g.:

- "I think the connection between us is very close. I have never had this happen before."

- "I have never shared their vision with me like you. We are destined to be together."

They Let You Speak First

This is a popular strategy that has individual business relationships, but it can also happen in personal relationships. When a person wants to establish control, they may ask exploratory questions to share your thoughts and concerns as early as possible. Given their hidden agenda, they can use your answers to manipulate your decision.

E.g.:

- "Oh my God, I never heard good news about that company. What is your experience?"

- "Well, you just require to explain why you are angry with me again."

They Distort the Facts

Emotional manipulators are masters who are good at using lies, or false statements to change reality to confuse you. They may exaggerate events and make themselves look more vulnerable. They may also underestimate their role in the conflict to win your sympathy.

E.g.:

- "I asked a question about the project, then she came to me and shouted that I had never done anything to help her, but you know what I did, right?"
- "I cried all night without blinking."

They Engage in Intellectual Bullying

If someone overwhelms you with statistics, technical terms, or facts when asking questions, you may be experiencing emotional manipulation. Some manipulators are assumed to be experts, and they impose "knowledge" on you. This is especially common in financial or sales situations.

E.g.:

- "You are a novice, so I don't want you to understand."
- "I know these have a lot of numbers for you, so that I will do it slowly again."

They Engage in Bureaucratic Bullying

Also, in a business environment, emotional manipulators may overwhelm you with paperwork, red tape, procedures, or anything that might hinder you. If you indicate to check carefully or raise questions that suspect its shortcomings or weaknesses, this is a distinct possibility.

E.g.:

- "This is too difficult for you. I will stop now and save my energy."
- "You are completely unaware of the headaches you have created for yourself."

Do You Feel Sorry for Expressing Your Doubts

If you ask questions or make suggestions, the emotional manipulator may react aggressively or lead you into an argument. This strategy allows them to control their choices and influence your decisions. They may also use this situation to make you feel inside by expressing your doubts first.

E.g.:

- "I don't understand why you don't trust me."
- "You know I'm just an anxious person. I'm useless, and I won't always know where you are."

They Reduced Your Problems and Played Their Part

If your day is terrible, emotional manipulators may take this opportunity to ask their questions.

The goal is to invalidate what you are experiencing so that you are forced to focus on them and exert emotional energy on their problems.

E.g.:

- "Do you think this is bad? You don't have to deal with the cube partner who has been talking on the phone."
- "Thank you for having a brother. I have been alone all my life."

Conclusion

From the above content, I concluded that you could get a thorough understanding of dark psychology, neural language programming (NLP), and manipulation. Dark psychology attempts to understand the system of thoughts, perceptions, and personal processing leading to predatory behavior contrary to the modern understanding of human behavior. It embraces all the people who connect us to the dark side. It suggests that we all have the potential for a predator's behavior, and it can penetrate thoughts, feelings, and perceptions.

The mechanism of psychopathy includes psychological, neurological, and biochemical behaviors. The most common signs of psychopathy involve irresponsible social behavior, ignore or violate the rights of others, cannot distinguish rights of others, delicately showing sympathy, manipulating or hurting others, general disregard for safety and recurring law problems.

Narcissism is a concept in psychoanalysis theory. It is the pursuit of vain worship of idealized self-image and traits. Narcissists exaggerate self-importance, unable to recognize the feelings of others, extreme jealousy, focus on fantasy, arrogant behavior. People with narcissistic personality disorder fall in love with the idealized grand image. Narcissist personality disorder involves self-centered patterns, arrogant thinking, and action, lack of empathy and consideration for others, and the great need for admiration. High self-awareness, living in a fantasy world, need constant praise and admiration, sense of right, use others without guilt, often belittle and intimidate others. Do not be obsessed with fantasy because narcissists can be very attractive and charming. There are many ways of leaving a narcissist, such as ending an abusive relationship, educate yourself about narcissistic personality disorder.

Machiavellianism is one of the characteristics of the so-called 'dark triad.' It is a personality trait that is a person they will manipulate, deceive and use others to achieve goals. People with characteristics of Machiavellianism tend to focus only on their ambitions and interests. They put money and power above all relationships, use others for success, low compassions and lack of enthusiasm in social interaction.

Neural Language Programming is a pseudo-scientific method for communication and personal development. There is some critical use case of NLP (NLP in neural machine translation), neural language processing in sentiment analysis, NLP human resources and recruitment, NLP in advertising, NLP in healthcare. NLP techniques can change by determining your emotions that you want to get rid of, encounter the whole situation from the observer's perspective.

Body language or nonverbal communication uses physical actions, facial expressions and manners to communicate nonverbally, usually instinctively rather than consciously.

Nonverbal communication is based on biology, while verbal communication is based on cultures. Nonverbal communication can play five roles (repetition, contradiction, substitution, supplement, and stress). The facial expressions, body movement, gestures, eye contact, touch, space and voice are nonverbal communication types. You can control your nonverbal communication by managing stress and by developing emotional awareness. You can read the body language by paying attention to inconsistencies, treating nonverbal communication signals as a whole and trusting your instincts. You can use nonverbal communication for modifying voice, replace speech, control dialogue, convey personality, status, expressions and emotions. You can improve the nonverbal communication skills by watching out for nonverbal signals, looking for inconsistent behavior, focusing on tone when speaking, using good eye contact and considering the context.

Mind control is a long process that gradually changes the victim's mind. Mind control transfers a process in which individuals or groups use the unethical manipulation methods to persuade others to obey wishes which harm the man being manipulated. NLP's mind control provides practical ways to change the way you think, view past events and process your life. Subconscious thought control skills (visualization, meditation, mirror talk, self-hypnosis) are some mind-control techniques for a better experience. NLP improves work efficiency by setting goals, improving employee's morale, better communication, learning development and changing behavior.

Hypnosis is a state similar to sleep, and during it, you will enter in a more focused and attentive state. Hypnosis can use to treat various diseases (gastrointestinal diseases, skin diseases and chronic pain), conditions and discomforts. Hypnosis techniques include relaxation techniques, handshake techniques, eyeball cue, visualization, arm levitation technology, sudden shock or regression, fixed eyes, body scan, countdown breathing, nonverbal communication, hypnosis advice, indirect suggestion, direct suggestion, hypnosis trigger, nonverbal communication, cold reading, warm reading, popular reading and swish model.

One of the effective ways to hypnotize someone is to enter the mind with the eyes. You can captivate through eyes by maintaining eye contact for a long time without blinking, practicing the ability to focus on the eyes, and increasing your awareness of peripheral devices. For hypnotizing, you should ask for permission, let the person sit in a comfortable upright position, tell the person that you are going to touch his shoulder, tell them its time to relax, set them to listen only to your voice.

Hypnosis can help you solve the six common health problems (insomnia, anxiety, irritable bowel syndrome symptoms, chronic pain, quitting smoking and losing weight). Hypnotherapy is a form of psychotherapy used to relax the patients during the consultation process. Hypnotherapy can treat diseases like phobia, addiction, relationship conflict, anxiety, depression and post-traumatic disorder. Potential risks of hypnotherapy include headache, dizziness, drowsiness, anxiety, distress and wrong memory creation.

Brainwashing is a severe form of social impact that can lead to changes in someone's way of thinking. The brainwasher will actively destroy the target's identity and replace it with another set of behaviors, attitudes and feelings. Singing, isolation, defense and fear, activity teaching methods, lack of sleep and fatigue, self-criticism and blame, love bombing, mysterious manipulation, brutal abuse and contemplative clichés are some brainwashing techniques.

If you want to understand how to brainwash someone, you will recognize the process they use to recruit new friends, change their attitudes and beliefs and involve them. Fear and inwardness are the two primary emotions used to control people under emotional control. Fear of outsiders, fear of rejection by the team, fear of losing, the anxiety of independent thinking and fear of leaving are everyday things that make people obey. You do not fall into the trap, avoid turning as much as possible, avoid emotional attachment, meditate often, let go of toxic relationships are many ways of protecting yourself from emotional manipulation. You can beat a manipulator by clarifying your wishes, watch resources and pay attention to their actions, not words.